Chinese Innovation
and Branding Leaps

Series on Innovation and Knowledge Management

Series Editor: Suliman Hawamdeh   **ISSN: 1793-1533**
            (University of North Texas)

*The complete list of the published volumes in the series can be found at
http://www.worldscientific.com/series/sikm

Series on Innovation and Knowledge Management – Vol. 16

Chinese Innovation and Branding Leaps

Edited by

Serdar S. Durmusoglu
China Jiliang University, China

 **World Scientific**

NEW JERSEY · LONDON · SINGAPORE · BEIJING · SHANGHAI · HONG KONG · TAIPEI · CHENNAI · TOKYO

Published by

World Scientific Publishing Co. Pte. Ltd.

5 Toh Tuck Link, Singapore 596224

USA office: 27 Warren Street, Suite 401-402, Hackensack, NJ 07601

UK office: 57 Shelton Street, Covent Garden, London WC2H 9HE

Library of Congress Cataloging-in-Publication Data
Names: Durmusoglu, Serdar S., editor.
Title: Chinese innovation and branding leaps / edited by
    Serdar S. Durmusoglu, China Jiliang University, China.
Description: Hackensack, NJ : World Scientific Publishing, 2022. |
    Series: Series on innovation and knowledge management, 1793-1533 ; volume 16 |
    Includes bibliographical references and index.
Identifiers: LCCN 2021046873 | ISBN 9789811249624 (hardcover) |
    ISBN 9789811249631 (ebook) | ISBN 9789811249648 (ebook other)
Subjects: LCSH: Knowledge management--China. | Branding (Marketing)--China. |
    New products--China.
Classification: LCC HD30.2 .C47443 2022 | DDC 658.4/0380951--dc23/eng/20211104
LC record available at https://lccn.loc.gov/2021046873

British Library Cataloguing-in-Publication Data
A catalogue record for this book is available from the British Library.

For any available supplementary material, please visit
https://www.worldscienti ic.com/worldscibooks/10.1142/12651#t=suppl

Desk Editors: Nimal Koliyat/Sandhya Venkatesh

Typeset by Stallion Press
Email: enquiries@stallionpress.com

Printed in Singapore

Dedicated to my mom

About the Editor

After getting his Ph.D. degree from Michigan State University, **Prof. Dr. Serdar S. Durmusoglu** earned his tenure and spent a total of more than a decade in academia in the United States. Several years ago, he moved to East Asia and since then, he has been working both in Thailand and in China in various positions at universities. Currently, he is a Professor of Marketing at China Jiliang University in Hangzhou, Zhejiang, China. He is also an editorial board member of the *Industrial Marketing Management* Journal. Within innovation, Professor Durmusoglu's main research areas are new product development (NPD) strategy and product innovation decisions, the interaction of NPD teams with other departments internally and externally with stakeholders, the effect of information technology on NPD, and open innovation. His works have been published in the top journals of his field such as *The Journal of Product and Innovation Management, Industrial Marketing Management, Journal of Knowledge Management, R&D Management*, and *Journal of Product and Brand Management*. He is also a co-editor of Product Development Management Association's (PDMA) book,

New Product Development Essentials: Tools for Open Innovation. Further, Dr. Durmusoglu is a member of PDMA's Outstanding Corporate Innovator Award Committee, an award that has been honoring corporations with extraordinary and sustained innovation practices for the past three and a half decades. Professor Durmusoglu can best be reached at sabbaticalserdar@ outlook.com.

About the Contributors

Yaman Alpata is the Country Manager of Turkey, Middle East and North Africa, and Latin America and Mexico for AliExpress, Alibaba Group in China (suleymanyaman.sy@alibaba-inc.com).

Junsong Chen is Professor of Marketing and the Dean at the School of Intelligent Finance and Business, Xi'an Jiaotong-Liverpool University (junsong.chen@xjtlu.edu.cn). His research interests lie in the areas of marketing, innovation, branding, and decision-making. He has published in many leading international journals including *International Journal of Research in Marketing, Journal of Business Ethics, Industrial Marketing Management, European Journal of Marketing, Journal of Business Research, Journal of World Business*, and *Journal of Marketing Management*. He is the author of the book *Marketing Management in Asia*, and has 15 marketing cases published in Europe Case Clearing House.

Rodney A. Josephson is an experienced serial entrepreneur with over three decades of business start-ups, marketing, business development and cross-cultural training, lecturing, and consulting experience (rodney. josephson@hotmail.com). Most of his work has been in Europe, North America, and East Asia, specifically in China. He has worked with some of the leading companies and educational institutions in his career, specializing in communication and linguistics matters.

Howard Pong Yuen Lam is the Director of Executive MBA Program and Associate Professor of Practice in Marketing at The Chinese University of Hong Kong (CUHK) Business School (lampongyuen@cuhk.edu.hk). Before joining the academia, he was head of marketing or general manager with rich commercial experience and a track record of sustained leadership and innovation for over 25 years. He had worked at P&G, McDonald's, Coca-Cola, and other multinational companies. His research studies were published in the *Journal of Marketing, Business Horizons, Journal of Database Marketing and Customer Strategy Management, Journal of the Operational Research Society*, and *Cornell Hotel and Restaurant Administration Quarterly*. To enhance course relevancy and practicality, he also conducted case research with co-authors and got business cases published by Ivey case center and listed at Harvard case center.

Sai Lan is Associate Professor of Innovation & Entrepreneurship at Emlyon Business School, Asia Campus, Academic Director of Executive Development Program ED, and Associate Operation Director of Business Intelligence Center (lan@em-lyon.com). Lan's research interests focus on innovation and entrepreneurship, with special emphasis on digital platform and open-source software ecosystems. Lan has published over 30 research papers in peer-reviewed academic journals, books, and major academic conferences, including a Best Paper Award in Academy of Management Annual Conference 2015. Lan also has extensive industry experience: as senior software engineer for Motorola and other technology companies in the US.

Kun Liu earned his Ph.D. in strategic management at the University of Utah (kliu10@kent.edu). Liu is currently an Assistant Professor of entrepreneurship at Kent State University. He is interested in digital platforms, innovation, initial public offering, and entrepreneurship. He has published in *Strategic Management Journal, Journal of Management, Research Policy*, among other journals.

Shiyu (Tracy) Lu is a Research Assistant Professor at Sau Po Centre on Ageing, The University of Hong Kong (sylu@hku.hk). Her research interests include health care policy, long-term care service, and age-friendly city.

Yuefang Si is an Associate Professor and the Head in the Department of Economic Geography, School of Urban & Regional Sciences, East China Normal University (yfsi@re.ecnu.edu.cn). She is the consultant of Trade, Investment and Innovation Division, ESCAP, UN for the project Science, Technology and Innovation Parks in Asia and Pacific Area. Her research interests include firm/region innovation, Chinese outward FDI, offshoring R&D and high-tech parks, etc. Her work widely appears in peer-reviewed journals such as *Technovation, Technology Analysis & Strategic Management, Asian Journal of Technology Innovation, Growth and Change, Journal of Contemporary China,* and *Tijdschrift voor Economische en Sociale Geografie,* among many others.

Cassandra Chen Wang is Professor in the School of Earth Sciences, Zhejiang University (chencwang@zju.edu.cn). Her research interests include trans-boundary knowledge/technology spillovers and firm innovation, industrial cluster and regional economies, e-commerce adoption and rural development. She is the author of *Upgrading China's Information and Communication Technology Industry: State-Firm Strategic Coordination and the Geography of Technological Innovation.* Her work widely appears in the peer-reviewed international journals such as *Journal of Economic Geography, Economic Geography, International Business Review, Environment and Planning A, Urban Studies, Journal of Rural Studies, Asia Pacific Viewpoint,* among many others. She is the principal investigator of three national research projects granted by National Science Foundation of China and is the recipient of Regional Studies Association Early Career Grant.

Vincent Chi Wong is Assistant Professor of Marketing at the City University of Hong Kong (vc.wong@cityu.edu.hk). His research interests include consumer information processing, cross-cultural consumer psychology, and marketing communications. His research has been published in top-tier psychology and business journals, such as *Journal of Personality* *and Social Psychology, Journal of Experimental Psychology: General, Journal of Consumer Research, Journal of Marketing Research,* and *Journal of Marketing.* Prior to his academic career. Vincent had been a radio and TV financial program host/anchor/producer in Hong Kong and Macau for years.

Jia Zhang is a Ph.D. student in the Melbourne School of Design, The University of Melbourne (jz6@student.unimelb.edu.au). Her research interests cover the e-commerce adoption and rural development, urban planning, as well as economic and urban geography. Her work has been published by various journals, including *Journal of Rural Studies, Progress in Geography,* and *Geographical Research.* Prior to undertaking her Ph.D., she obtained her master's degree from Zhejiang University under the supervision and guidance of Professor Cassandra Wang.

Contents

1

Chinese Innovation and Branding Leaps: Introduction

Serdar S. Durmusoglu

A previous volume of the Series on Innovation and Knowledge Management discussed managing organizational complexities in the rapidly developing Chinese market through case studies of many leading firms such as Haier, China Mobile, and Damai.[1] This volume primarily takes a different look at China and focuses on providing conceptual and empirical (both case-based and survey-based) studies on the challenges faced and lessons learned regarding the "management of innovation, knowledge management, and branding" by Chinese firms in the global arena. In that regard, I hope this book highlights some of the recent innovations and branding efforts by leading and emerging Chinese firms. As many of us spending considerable time in Asia and China are surprisingly aware, many Western business and political leaders still seem to wrongly view and/or portray China as the world's manufacturing district as well as a heaven for

---

[1]Damai is a comprehensive entertainment brand in Mainland China and primarily sells concert, sports events, and theater tickets.

1

copycat products. Furthermore, this book also aims to assist foreign firms as they are introducing new products and managing their branding efforts in Chinese markets.

Experiences of Chinese firms in the world arena and foreign firms in China are crucial since China is not only the largest emerging market, but also the second-largest economy in the world. As such, while Chinese firms are trying to penetrate more markets globally, many foreign firms are hoping to get a piece of the fast-growing Chinese markets. In fact, recent estimates show that more than a third of China's population (close to 500 million consumers) will be upper middle-income or high-income consumers by 2030.[2] Furthermore, as Sheth (2011) argues, emerging markets possess very different characteristics, chronic shortage of resources, and unbranded competition among others. Correspondingly, firms from emerging markets lack international marketing experience and own brands with low brand equities (Ramamurti and Williamson 2019). As a result, we should examine firms operating in and from these markets diligently and rethink existing scholarly thought as well as common practices of marketing.

The target audience for this volume is both new and experienced innovation and branding managers operating in China and from China, as well as managers contemplating ways to expand their product innovation reach across the globe, build long-lasting brands, or protect and enhance their existing brand image and equity. Given the cut-throat competitive nature of innovation and branding, I hope that this book fulfills a need and demonstrates numerous keys to success and some pitfalls to avoid in such tumultuous journeys.

All chapters contain examples of firms, products, or brands that have either enjoyed successes or learned significantly from their mistakes in innovation and/or branding. I therefore expect the readers to significantly benefit from these experiences described. I open the book with a chapter authored by Si and colleagues, where the focus is on information and communication technology (ICT) adoption and product innovation by Chinese firms. The authors describe how and to what extent ICT adoption that enhances firm innovation should be thoroughly investigated and then

---

[2] See The Economist Intelligence Unit report "The Chinese Consumer in 2030" for details.

report on their investigation of how ICT use for both intra-firm operation and inter-firm relations in Chinese manufacturing firms enhance firm innovation. They also provide an excellent historical overview of the growth and spatial distribution of ICT use across China. As a result, their chapter should not only aid Chinese firms when contemplating advanced ICTs to facilitate their businesses but also firms in many other emerging countries with ambitions of ICT leaps as well.

In Chapter 3, Sai and his colleagues discuss the past, present, and future of open-source software platform innovations in China. As the open-source software ecosystem has become a dynamic innovation environment in high technology industries and many Chinese firms are now sponsoring or supporting open-source software platforms, the authors examine the knowledge strategy types associated with open-source software. They also underline the unique aspects of open-source innovations in China, give detailed examples from leading firms such as Huawei, and conclude their chapter with lessons learned. In this regard, this chapter will both give firms from all over the world an update on the fast-developing open-source software activity in China, and also provide guidance on how to manage fast-emerging open-source software systems.

Chapter 4 is a treatise on the localization of cross-border services by global business-to-consumer (B2C) platforms. The chapter is based on the journey of AliExpress, particularly its experience of entering Turkey and enabling many Turkish small- and medium-sized enterprises (SMEs) becoming successful globally. Starting with a short overview of Alibaba, followed by AliExpress' milestones, the authors describe how AliExpress enables local brands to succeed in e-commerce. The chapter concludes with a brief guide to effectively localizing a global cross-border e-commerce marketplace.

Next, in Chapter 5, Lam and his colleagues present the results of branding strategies for new product launches. Specifically, they delve into whether firms in China create corporate name or product brand names from English to Chinese based on phonetic, semantic, and phono-semantic methods or create names with suggestive meanings. They also investigate whether firms should use one name as both corporate name and product brand name or should they create two names with two different meanings. This chapter is full of examples from the past and the present and is valuable to firms contemplating on how to enter into Chinese markets with their existing brands.

Lam and other colleagues examine the branding issues in China from a different lens in Chapter 6: corporate branding strategies firms should follow. They provide many examples as well, particularly, how two start-ups from Hong Kong S.A.R., namely, GoGoVan and LaLaMove and their brands progressed over the years. I believe that the readers will find many usable tools and ideas to assist in their branding strategies of their firms.

In the last chapter, Josephson describes ways of using neuro-linguistic programming (NLP) to build Chinese brands and mainly focuses how NLP can help SMEs. In addition to introducing how NLP be deployed in branding, the author also delineates in topics such as etymology, psychology, and cultural characteristics that affect how the consumer processes and perceives messages based on their senses and how these messages gain meaning in consumers' long-term memories.

I am grateful to have these exceptionally talented group of scholars and managers to contribute to this book and truly appreciate their eagerness to share their experiences, studies, and thoughts on a wide variety of topics in innovation and branding (I am also thankful to Professor Suliman Hawamdeh of University of North Texas for his feedback when choosing a title for this book, Professor Suli Zheng of China Jiliang University and Professor Regina C. McNally of Saint Xavier University for their feedback on the chapters I authored and co-authored). That said, I encourage scholars to continue conducting more detailed case studies on successful brands and innovations from China. For successful brand building case studies, Anta Sports Products' or Bosideng's journeys or case studies of shortcuts to brand building such as brand acquisitions of FILA and MG, and joint ventures such as the Sino-Swedish venture Polestar can be investigated. Building successful Chinese brands in other emerging markets (e.g., Transsion in Africa or Oppo and Vivo in ASEAN countries) should be explored as well because different capabilities may be necessary than building brand equity in the West. Future studies should also focus on this aspect to obtain a more granular view.

For a successful innovation, the development of COMAC C919 can be explored. COMAC C919 is manufactured by Comac, which is a Chinese state-owned aerospace manufacturer in Shanghai. In 2008, the development program of the single-aisle twinjet C919 started in 2008 and the initial prototype was completed in 2015. Recently, Airbus' CEO argued that COMAC's C919 will be a formidable competition for the Airbus by the end of this decade (Bodell 2021). Regarding innovation, future research should examine the differing approaches of firms in China and elsewhere for revolutionizing electric vehicle industries. For example, a comparison of Shanghai-based Nio, which is now worth more than General Motors despite almost going bankrupt in 2020, and the American firm Tesla would be valuable.

There are many unexplored aspects of Chinese innovation and branding leaps. For example, future research can investigate how innovation parks facilitate innovations by Chinese firms. These parks operate in many top-tier as well as mid-tier cities and some have incubated or accelerated many star Chinese firms already. Future research should document the operational differences and lessons learned from these parks.

While some of the chapters in this book discuss what it might take for a Chinese brand to succeed in the West, as we have seen in the case of TikTok, the journey only beings when a Chinese brand becomes a hit in the West. There will be other hurdles to overcome such as governmental regulations or significantly different consumer protection policies elsewhere in the world. Nevertheless, I hope that this book sheds some light on recent innovation and branding leaps from China, encourages scholars to examine these issues in more detail, and assists managers in their journey for doing sterling work in innovation and branding!

References

Bodell, L. (2021). Airbus is confident COMAC's C919 can compete against the A320neo. Retrieved on May 17, 2021. https://simpleflying.com/airbus-comac-a320neo-competition, *Marketing News*, 2017, August Issue, 35–36.

Sheth, J. N. (2011). Impact of emerging markets on marketing: Rethinking existing perspectives and practices, *Journal of Marketing*, 75(July), 166–182.

Ramamurti, R. and Williamson, P. J. (2019). Rivalry between emerging-market MNEs and developed-country MNEs: Capability holes and the race to the future, *Business Horizons*, 62, 157–169.

© 2022 World Scientific Publishing Company
https://doi.org/10.1142/9789811249631_0002

ICT Adoption and Product Innovation of Chinese Firms: A Perspective on Intra- and Inter-firm Operations

Yuefang Si, Cassandra C. Wang, and Jia Zhang

1. Introduction

During the past 30 years, information and communication technologies (ICT) have been diffusing globally in practically all sectors of the economy due to its broad spectrum of applications. The adoption and use of ICT in business has fundamentally increased the efficiency and enhanced the competitiveness of firms (Brynjolfsson and Hitt 2003; Reeson and Rudd 2016; Sambamurthy and Subramani 2005). The digital economy has induced a plenty of studies on ICT adoption of firms. Durmusoglu and Barczak (2011) collected data from new product development managers in the US and Canada. Barczak *et al.* (2008) compared the relationships between IT usage and new product performance in two different countries — the United States and the Netherlands. Bertschek *et al.* (2013) provided evidence from German firms for the impact of broadband

Internet on firms' product innovation. Ollo-López and Aramendia-Muneta (2012) used data from the survey conducted in six European countries (France, Germany, Italy, Spain, and United Kingdom).

These studies are all conducted in developed economies with little attention to developing economies (see Gallego *et al.* 2015 for an exception — they examined firms in a developing country, namely, Colombia). Therefore, there is a gap in the body of knowledge in this area. In this study, we fill this gap by exploring the application of ICT to both internal operations and external inter-firm relations and their subsequent impact on firm innovation, with a sample of manufacturing firms from China.

In addition to being a developing country, investigation of this phenomenon in the Chinese context is important for another reason as well: China has transformed itself from one of the poorest countries to the world's second-largest economy and the first-ever middle-income country to join the world's top 25 innovative economies in 2016 (Cornell University *et al.* 2016). According to the latest data, China ranks 14th among the 131 economies featured in the Global Innovation Index (Cornell University *et al.* 2020). Thus, China provides a highly interesting setting for examining the role of ICT adoption in firm innovation performance in emerging countries.

Extant research on China's innovation gives much emphasis upon external technology transfer from foreign investment (Hempell *et al.* 2004; Morikawa 2004; Thompson 2002; Young and Lan 2010), as well as internal investment in human capital and R&D activities on indigenous innovation (Fu *et al.* 2010; Tang and Hussler 2011).

Among the few studies in the Chinese context, Meng and Li (2002) provided empirical evidence on China's ICT industry development and ICT diffusion in the 1990s. Furthermore, Skoko *et al.* (2008) developed a model of ICT adoption of Chinese SMEs from different industrial sectors to present that the adoption and use of ICT are the fundamental source of competitiveness. Sun *et al.* (2017) explored how ICT stimulates innovation performance through interactions within in-house R&D investment and external technology purchase. However, neither of them has analyzed the different mechanism and results of ICT adoption in internal business activities, or in external relationships with partners and customers, from whom firms are able to acquire valuable knowledge for innovation.

The remainder of this chapter is structured as follows. In the next section, we illustrate the historical development and geographical distribution of ICT infrastructure and innovation performance at the provincial level in China. Next, we review the literature on the ICT adoptions and innovative performance of firms before we develop our hypotheses for the study. This is followed by a clarification of our own data source and research design. Attention is then turned to the empirical analyses of the impact of ICT adoption on product innovation of Chinese firms in Section 5. Findings of this research and their theoretical and managerial implications are summarized and discussed in the end.

2. Growth and Spatial Distribution of ICT Uses in China

2.1. *Historical development of ICT adoption in China*

Over the last three decades, China's ICT industry has been one of the most rapidly expanding industrial sectors in the country and in the world. The Chinese government views ICT not only as a cutting-edge industry for China's transition from a manufacturing to a knowledge-based economy but also a significant technology that promotes the growth and innovation of the entire society (Atkinson 2014). However, the development of China's ICT infrastructure is only a recent phenomenon, with its dramatic growth supported by the state during the last decade.

Figure 1 shows the national popularization rates of telephone and Internet in the past 20 years. Before 2000, the popularization rate of telephone was below 20 pieces per 100 persons and Internet was barely used. Since 2001, the year China joined the World Trade Organization (WTO), the popularization rate of telephone has been continuously increasing with a rate of 10% every year. At the end of 2012, each person in China at least owned one telephone on average. A similar pattern can be found with the case of the Internet. Not until the year of 2006 when General Office of the Communist Party of China Central Committee and General Office of the State Council released a document titled "State Informatization Development Strategy (2006–2020)" to promote a wide use of Internet, did the Internet applications achieve a rapid growth. Moreover, the relative importance of Internet compared to telephone as a communication

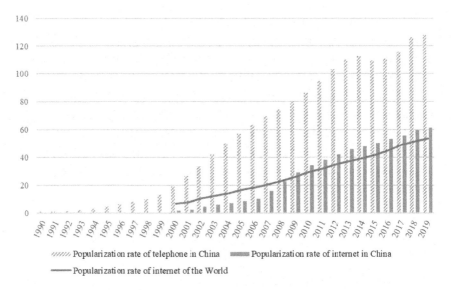

Figure 1. Growth of the adoption of telephone and Internet in China and globally, 1990–2019.

Data source: Popularization rate of telephone and Internet are calculated from China Statistic Year book at various years, and the global Internet usage information comes from the International Telecommunication Union.

channel has consistently increased. In 2009, the popularization rate of Internet in China exceeded the global average level, and has maintained a leading position since then. Nowadays, both telephone and Internet have become an indispensable part of people's life in China.

2.2. *Spatial distribution of ICT adoption in China*

The use of telephone and the Internet in China is characterized by an extreme regional variation and unevenness. As shown in Figure 2, the 31 provincial units in China can be simply categorized into four tiers. Beijing and Shanghai are in the first tier with their popularization rate in terms of both telephone and Internet strikingly higher than other regions. This is followed by Zhejiang and Guangdong where their popularization rate is more than 0.99 standard deviation of the national average. Tianjin and Fujian can be categorized into the second tier in terms of Internet use but they are counted into the third tier for telephone use. These regions are

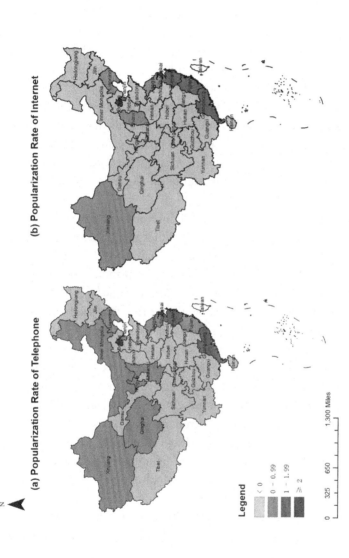

Figure 2. Spatial distribution of the use of telephone and Internet at the provincial level, 2011.

Note: Popularization rate of telephone/Internet refers to the ratio of the subscribers of telephone/number of cyber citizens to total population at the provincial level. This figure is calculated on the basis of the mean and standard deviation. For instance, the interval 0–0.99 in the legend indicates that the values are within 1 standard deviation of the mean.

Data source: Calculated from NBSC (2012).

economically advanced and innovation-intensive with a geographical agglomeration of the ICT manufacturing activities (Wang and Lin 2010; Warner 2015). The third tier consists of regions with their popularization rate slightly higher than the national average, such as, Liaoning, Jiangsu, and Xinjiang. Xinjiang has a high popularization rate of Internet even though it is neither highly industrialized/economically developed nor ICT and innovation-intensive. One potential explanation is that the Internet is a more convenient way to gain information for the people in Xinjiang, which is vast and sparsely populated. Inner Mongolia shows a higher rate of telephone use, but a lower rate of Internet use than the national average. In contrast, Shanxi province presents an opposite pattern. Most of the western and middle regions fall into the fourth tier with a low rate of telephone and Internet use, including Heilongjiang, Jilin, Hebei, Henan, and Hubei.

We further investigate telephone and Internet use in the 25 cities which were selected by World Bank for the Enterprises Survey. As shown in Figure 3, cities in Pearl River Delta (Guangzhou, Shenzhen, and Dongguan), Yangtze River Delta (Shanghai, Hangzhou, and Ningbo), Beijing, and Tianjin present a higher ratio of telephone and Internet use than others. This finding is consistent with the research made by World Economic Forum *et al.* (2016) that China's three biggest and prosperous metropolises, namely National Capital Region of China, the Pearl River Delta, and the Yangtze River Delta in the coastal regions, have a popularization rate as high as that of the technologically advanced G7 countries.[1] The strikingly high rate of ICT use in these cities result not only from the rapid economic growth and local government support but also from the promotion of several ICT-related leading companies. For example, Beijing, Shanghai–Hangzhou, Shenzhen–Guangzhou–Dongguan harbored the biggest ICT equipment providers, including Huawei, ZTE, and Lenovo, and attracted the most influential e-commerce and online service companies, such as, Alibaba and Tencent. The headquarters of three biggest telecom service providers, namely China Telecom, China Unicom, and China Mobile are also located in these cities. These ICT giants are

---

[1]G7 countries are Canada, France, Germany, Italy, Japan, the United Kingdom, and the United States.

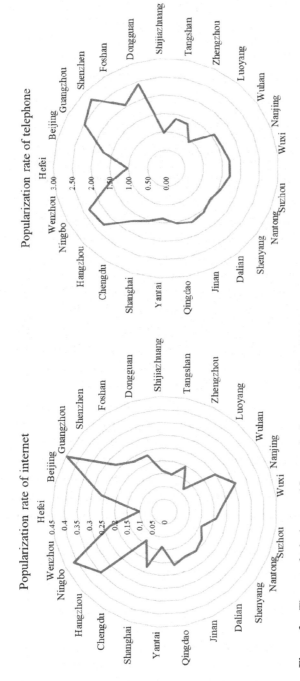

Figure 3.   The use of telephone and Internet in the sample cities, 2011.

Note: Popularization rate of telephone/Internet refers to the ratio of the subscribers of telephone/Internet access to total population in a city.

Data source: Calculated from NBSC (2012).

believed to promote the wide use of ICT not only in households but also enterprises (Meng and Li 2002; Wu and Zhang 2010).

2.3. *Evolution of ICT adoption by Chinese firms*

Similar to the rapid growth of ICT adoption at the regional level, ICT adoption by firms has also developed dynamically in China. Technologically speaking, ICT adoption of Chinese firms has experienced four stages. As early as the 1970s, a number of large-sized Chinese firms, particularly state-owned enterprises, started to adopt single-computer ICT software, such as CAD and CAM, to promote the production efficiency. Since the mid-1980s, firms began to adopt local area network (LAN) systems to link different functional departments for internal data sharing and a better coordination of these departments. Firms also developed management information systems and office automation systems to optimize business processes and further increase efficiency. In the late 1990s, the process of informatization of Chinese firms accelerated with globalization and a wide use of Internet in China. Software such as ERP, supply chain management (SCM) and CRM systems, on the basis of the open and integrated wide area network (WAN) system were gradually introduced to Chinese firms (Xie 2000). In this stage, Chinese government initiated Gold Card,[2] Gold Bridge[3] and other national information technology projects to foster the ICT adoption of firms.

After 2000, another national information technology projects such as Golden Customers was initiated to encourage firms to adopt EDI. Not only big firms but also small- and medium-sized enterprises were motivated to apply ICT to routine operations. More and more firms started to set up Chief Information Office and IT division to facilitate the

---

[2]The Gold Card is a project started in June 1993 with the purpose of building a national credit card network. It uses bank cards as a medium to realize currency circulation in the form of electronic information transfer through computer network systems.

[3]The Gold Bridge project first announced in 1993. The backbones of this project are interconnected space satellite and ground fiber optic networks linked to a domestic private network. Apart from providing Internet access, the system allows email, electronic data interchange, database online services, information sources, and applications service systems.

informatization of the whole firms. ERP, CRM, product life-cycle management (PLM), business process management (BPM), and other integrated management software of business processes are increasingly used to enhance the knowledge management of firms. Internet+, SAAS cloud, and other technologies are developed to improve the efficiency of communications with suppliers and customers.

Figure 4 gives a brief summary of the evolution of ICT adoption by Chinese firms from 1970s to 2000s. The scope of ICT adoption has been extended from intra-firm level to inter-firm level during this period. Before the 1980s, ICT software, such as CAD and CAM, was applied at the department level. The 1990s witnessed the popular use of ERP and other more advanced software at the firm level (Beijing CCID Publishing, Media Co., 2011). At the same time, software such as SCM and CRM was used to manage inter-firm relationships. Since then, ICT has been more widely and deeply applied to both intra-firm operations and inter-firm relationships. Moreover, the continuous penetration and adoption of Internet create the basis for continual advances with respect to e-commerce in the digital economy.

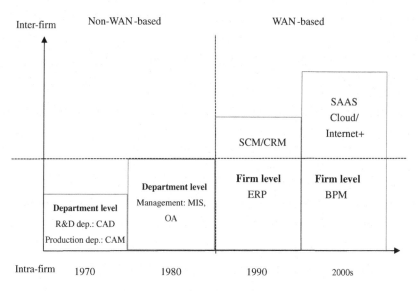

Figure 4.　Evolution of ICT adoption by Chinese firms.

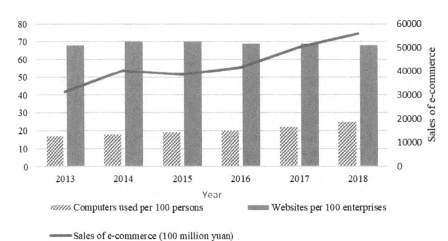

Figure 5. Informatization and e-commerce of manufacturing enterprises, China.
Data source: National Bureau of Statistic of China.

The advanced e-commerce capabilities in integrating and coordinating the material, information, and financial flows of all links in supply chain further strengthen the management capabilities of enterprises (Kraemer *et al.* 2005). As can be seen from Figure 5, manufacturing enterprises in China move toward increasing use of online tools for conducting business and information acquisition. Anhui Heli is an example of such a company. Anhui Heli is one of the leading enterprises in China's industrial vehicle industry. The main product of Anhui Heli is forklift. Although it became one of the top 10 industrial vehicle industries in the world since 2006, Anhui Heli had also faced a series of problems, such as a lack of effective management of product life cycle, a lack of intelligence and visualization of supply chain planning and production execution, and the lack of overall collaborative management of supply chain. After that, Anhui Heli built an Integrated Product Development (IPD) system; built a product life-cycle management platform that runs through research, production, supply, and marketing; built a sales system covering all sales outlets through ERP and VMS; built a data sharing platform to achieve cross-post and cross-department data transmission. The adoption of these ICTs has had an instant influence on firm's activities. The manufacturing cycle of the firm is reduced by 45%, the product life-cycle management

Table 1. The purpose of Internet use by surveyed firms.

	%
Sell and market products	89.86
Make purchase for this establishment	75.16
Do research and develop ideas on new goods and services	58.95

Data source: Calculated from Enterprises Survey of World Bank, 2012.

cost is reduced by 38%, the speed of product update is also greatly increased, and the average order delivery time is 30% faster than before.

After figuring out what types of ICT media have been used by Chinese firms, we further investigate the purpose that Chinese firms adopt ICT. The Enterprises Survey of World Bank provides useful information for this question (Table 1). Obviously, maintaining relationship with customers to sell and to market products is the most important reason as 90% of firms report that they adopt Internet for this purpose. Around 75% of Chinese firms adopt Internet in order to exchange information with suppliers to purchase goods and services. More than a half of firms use Internet to do research and develop new product ideas, which suggests that Internet application is directly related to innovation.

2.4. *Geographical patterns of innovation in China*

After examining the historical development and spatial distribution of ICT adoption in China, we now explore the geographical patterns of China's innovation activities at the provincial level. Since spatial autocorrelation method is widely used to analyze geographical characteristics (Bertazzon 2003; Melecky 2015), we employ local spatial autocorrelation method to detect the spatial correlation degree in terms of granted invention patents and new products between neighboring locations in Figure 6. HH/LL indicates that the high/low observation area is surrounded by high/low observation area, while LH indicates that the low observation area is surrounded by the high observation area. These three types of spatial agglomeration can reflect the spatial heterogeneity and instability in local regions.

As shown in Figure 6, the spatial distribution of granted invention patents and output of new products in China is not totally random.

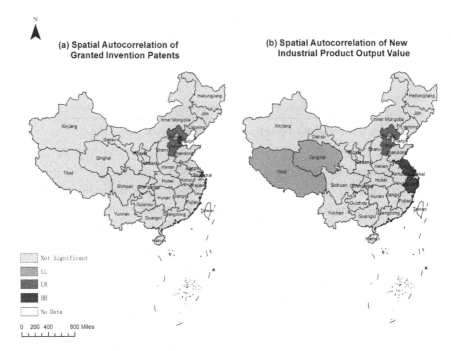

Figure 6. Spatial autocorrelation of granted invention patents and new industrial product output value at the provincial level, 2011.

Note: Spatial autocorrelation of granted invention patents refers to the ratio of the numbers of granted invention patents to total population at the provincial level. Spatial autocorrelation of new industrial product output value refers to the ratio of output value of new products of industry to Value-added of Industry at the provincial level. The local spatial autocorrelation is evaluated based on the local Moran index according to spatial neighboring relations.

Data source: Calculated from NBSC (2012).

In particular, two major economic regions, namely Shanghai–Jiangsu–Zhejiang and Beijing–Tianjin–Hebei, show a different innovation performance. In Shanghai–Jiangsu–Zhejiang region, Shanghai is the HH region which is evaluated by not only granted invention patents but also output of new products, whereas Zhejiang and Jiangsu are HH regions are evaluated only by output of new products. It indicates that Yangtze River Delta is in the process of innovation diffusion and therefore the region presents a relatively even geographical pattern of innovation. However, in Beijing–Tianjin–Hebei region, Hebei province is the LH region, namely, it is surrounded by regions with a high level of innovative performance.

It suggests that the innovation of Beijing is not yet spilled over to Hebei province. In the western area, Tibet and Qinghai are two LL regions as shown in Figure 6(a). This is not surprising that the western regions as a whole are less innovative than other regions. When comparing the regional ICT adoption in Figure 2 with the regional innovation performance in Figure 6, we find that the regions which have a high level of ICT adoption, such as Shanghai, Jiangsu, and Zhejiang, seem to have a better innovation performance. Therefore, we will further probe into the relationship between ICT adoption and innovation of Chinese firms in the following section to explore why and how ICT adoption influences firms' innovation performance at the firm level.

3. Literature Review: How Does ICT Adoption Influence Firm Innovation?

Technological innovation, as the engine of economic growth and the source of firm competitiveness, has attracted much academic attention from different research angles (Fagerberg *et al*. 2005). Among many others, internal inputs of firms, such R&D and high-qualified labors, along with external innovation network with related firms and organizations, are believed to be the fundamental elements that could enhance the innovative performance of firms (Wang and Lin 2013). It is not until very recently, however, that the adoption and use of ICT has been treated as a significant input which is in parallel with R&D and talents to technological innovation (Hall *et al*. 2013; Sun *et al*. 2017). Although extant studies have pointed to a significant relationship between ICT adoption and firm innovation, most of them are based on theoretical inference rather than empirical evidence, and none of them pays attention to the potentially heterogeneous impact on firm innovation exerted by ICT applications in different activities of value creation and in the maintenance of inter-firm relations with different agents. Being an internal input to innovation, ICT not only enables firms to directly apply it to internal production and operation for the purpose of innovation but also indirectly accelerates innovation through facilitating external linkages and communications for knowledge exchange and creation. Building upon the existing theoretical and empirical literature, this section unfolds the influential mechanism of ICT adoption on innovation by investigating the ICT use in both intra-firm business activities and inter-firm communication and relationships.

3.1. *ICT adoption in internal operations and firm innovation*

First of all, ICT applications to *research and development activities* or *product enhancement* will increase the probability of innovation. Product enhancement refers to the updating of products to retain its competitive edge, such as extending products capabilities, improving product's performance, and scalability. For instance, the use of computer-aided design (CAD) can increase the number of alternative designs considered, shorten the development cycle and spark the inspiration of engineers to design new products (Carbonara 2005). It is found that those firms using ICT in their R&D departments are 6% more likely to introduce new products than their counterparts without ICT applications (Higón 2012). By increasing design speed or allowing more precise and detailed design activities, ICTs have the potential to improve firms' innovation in multiple ways (Vaccaro *et al.* 2010). The ICT workflow that involves the establishment of predefined electronic processes can make technological process easier and more efficient to enhance organization learning and innovation (Lopez-Nicolas and Soto-Acosta 2010). ICT adoption allows R&D employees to access valuable knowledge more quickly, readily, and easily through the participation in discussion forums, which reduces R&D costs and facilitates innovation (Vu 2011). Wasko and Faraj (2005) also highlight that interactions through message posts in such forums can bind geographically dispersed and diverse members into a collective to help members solve problems faced in specific practice. As stated by Kawakami *et al.* (2015), more frequent use of various types of IT tools would allow people to interact continuously and improve the proficiency with which particular product innovation activities are undertaken. It is argued that knowledge management-related ICT empowers tacit and contextual knowledge to spread in a meaningful way, which is more valuable than codified knowledge and is always restrained within a bounded territorial system (Carbonara 2005).

Second, ICT uses in *production and operation* can reduce production costs, enhance production efficiency, and boost process innovation. It is believed that the use of computer-aided manufacturing (CAM), artificial intelligence, and dedicated software has revolutionized manufacturing industry by providing a transformation of unstructured complex processes into routinized ones, and hence a better control of productive process and a higher efficiency (Kossaï and Piget 2014). The use of Internet helps to shorten product development cycles, simplify the ordering process, shrink inventory and implement time-based competition (Mustaffa and Beaumont 2004; Durmusoglu and Barczak 2011). The applications of groupware technology and shared database can lead to changes in the sequence of tasks in a process and even allow multiple tasks to be worked simultaneously (Carbonara 2005). ICT also promotes cross-department collaboration and strengthens internal knowledge exchange to develop novel products or process innovation, which is especially important for multi-location enterprises (Higón 2012). Sørensen and Snis (2001) convey similar information that ICT is a critical success factor for organizations due to its importance in facilitating and encouraging the process of transmission and diffusion of knowledge for innovation throughout the entire organization. A case study of non-farm rural enterprises in a coastal region of China demonstrates that ICT-facilitated interactions enable rural enterprises to reach out to external information in a timely manner, and then they integrate the new knowledge into their knowledge base and apply it to designing new and innovative products (Zhou *et al.* 2019).

Thirdly, ICT use in *marketing and sales* is another source of firms' success and innovation (Vilaseca-Requena *et al.* 2007). The website of a company has been regarded as a marketing platform to raising firms' visibility and attracting new customers. In fact, a study informs that those firms holding a website are 8% more likely to innovate in new products and 6% more likely to introduce new or improved process (Higón 2012). It is suggested that IT tools, such as a website, can be a way to share good practices and explicit knowledge for marketing processes (Kawakami *et al.* 2011).

ICTs also enable firms to eliminate redundant process and remove unnecessary layers of value chain such as intermediary agents to establish direct interface with their upstream and downstream partners (Molla and Heeks 2007). By giving the firms a greater exposure to the world-wide high-qualified workforce, ICT applications permit the firms to seek out and recruit new innovative employees (Steinfield *et al.* 2010). The adoption of e-business can overcome the geographical barriers and time restrictions to expand the business boundaries of firms, reduce coordination and search costs, and offer new services and new ways to value creation (Fariselli *et al.* 1999; Steinfield and Scupola 2008). E-commerce also allows firms to develop massive database that covers customers' demographic and psychographic information. This type of information, along with the click stream counts and purchase records tracking, can be analyzed with data-mining software so as to create a personalized interface for a better advertising and to provide ideas for an enhancement of existing products and even developing new products to meet customers' requirements and expectations (Amit and Zott 2001). For example, Taobao (the biggest e-commerce platform in China) shopkeepers can use the "Tao data" software on Alibaba platform to analyze the transaction amount, the number of transaction users, the number of transactions, customer turnover rate and other data, and the results can be used to capture information related to customer preference and adjust the business strategy. The Internet and email systems provide firms excellent capability to target specific groups or individuals precisely and enable them to realize one-to-one marketing strategies and practice mass customization. When it comes to the decisions relevant to marketing and sales, ICT entails a speedy gathering and analyzing of competitive knowledge and market information to simplify the decision process (Vilaseca-Requena *et al.* 2007). Based upon the theoretical backdrop identified earlier, we hypothesize,

Hypothesis 1: ICT adoption in internal operations is positively associated with product innovation of firms.

Hypothesis 1a: ICT adoption in R&D activities or product enhancement is positively associated with product innovation of firms.

Hypothesis 1b: ICT adoption in production and operation is positively associated with product innovation of firms.

Hypothesis 1c: ICT adoption in sales and marketing is positively associated with product innovation of firms.

3.2. *ICT adoption in inter-firm relationship and firm innovation*

Firms cannot be innovative in isolation, but need to interact with external sources to obtain complementary knowledge and technology for innovation (Fagerberg 2005). Dong and Netton (2017) found that IT investment is a key input to building a knowledge network as it supports firms' open innovation initiatives through broadening the breadth and deepening the depth of external search. Partners, such as suppliers, would generally, have better expertise and a more comprehensive understanding of the supplied parts and components that are necessary to fix particular technical problems (Nieto and Santamaría 2007; Tsai 2009). Therefore, co-operation and linkages with partners enable firms to reduce lead times of product development and enhance flexibility, product quality, and market adaptability (Chung and Kim, 2003). Customers are believed to contribute greatly to innovation by providing their expertise and virtually integrating into a company's innovation process, which could provide valuable inputs for new product development (Dubiel *et al.* 2014).

As it stands, ICT can boost innovation by providing a worldwide connectivity in synchronous and asynchronous modes that facilitates inter-firm coordination and maintains frequent and close relations with their partners and customers on an unprecedented scale (Alam and Noor 2009; Venkatraman and Henderson 1998). The contribution of ICTs can be particularly significant for innovation in the context of inter-firm collaborative relationships, for example, the use of knowledge management tools (KMTs) can lead to effective inter-firm collaborations by improving the quality, depth, and easiness of knowledge exchange and spread (Vaccaro *et al.* 2010). E-commerce adoption ensures a real-time communication independent of geographical proximity among production and trading partners, which is even more timely and efficiently than face-to-face contacts (Wu *et al.* 2003). ICT media used for the relations with suppliers, partners and customers, such as e-mail, FAQ lists, discussion forums, online questionnaires, and chatting systems enrich the opportunities to obtain externally valuable inputs for sustained innovation. Nambisan and Baron (2009) identify benefits that individuals can derive from media usage, and they point out that not only firms are able to obtain cognitive benefits from the knowledge generated and shared through continuous customer interaction, customers also derive considerable pleasure from conversing with one another about the product. It is also claimed that ICT applications help firms understand customers' needs and requirements before their competitors to develop innovative products catering to new and existing market (Parida and Örtqvist 2015). By supporting a frequent and repetitive interaction, ICT-based communication creates an atmosphere of trust and commitment, and even forms a steady social link between agents that leads to a deepening of information and knowledge exchange (Vilaseca-Requena *et al.* 2007). Therefore, we propose the following hypotheses:

Hypothesis 2: The adoption of ICT in external relations can facilitate inter-firm knowledge exchange and hence enhance the product innovation of firms.

Hypothesis 2a: The adoption of ICT in external relations with partners can facilitate inter-firm knowledge exchange and hence enhance the product innovation of firms.

Hypothesis 2b: The adoption of ICT in external relations with customers can facilitate inter-firm knowledge exchange and hence enhance the product innovation of firms.

Figure 7 shows the mechanisms of how ICT applications to both internal operations and external inter-firm relationships enhance product innovation of firms. It is worth noting that we did not cover all types of ICT media in Figure 7, but only give several examples to illustrate their influence. We especially highlight the role played by relatively complicated ICT media in firm innovation. The next section will clarify the specific types of ICT media studied in this chapter.

4. Data and Methodology

The purpose of this study is essentially to probe into the mechanism of ICT adoption on firm innovation, with special attention paid to ICT use in internal activities and operations as well as external relationships with

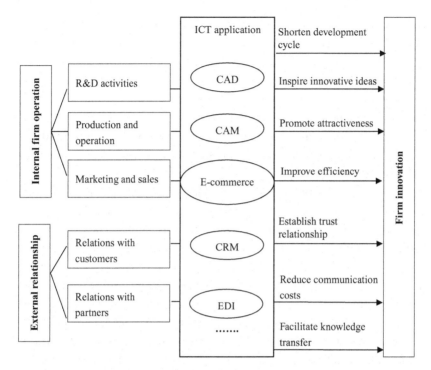

Figure 7. Map of the mechanism of ICT adoption on firm innovation.

partners and customers, especially in Chinese manufacturing firms. It also concerns with the issues about the types of ICT medium are used for inter-firm relationships and transactions, and the role played by these types of ICT in facilitating firm innovation.

Data used in this research are mainly derived from a large-scale firm-level questionnaire survey in China conducted by the World Bank. The Enterprise Survey of World Bank includes not only basic financial information of 1,692 manufacturing firms in China's 25 major cities which are either national centers such as Beijing, Shanghai, and Guangzhou or significant provincial centers like Shenzhen, Hangzhou, Nanjing, etc., but also information about their innovation performance, R&D activities and the extent of ICT applications that is particularly relevant to our study. The sample firms include both large-sized firms and small- and medium-sized firms, and the age of those firms is of great variety. We also collected data from China Statistic Yearbook and China City Statistic Yearbook to investigate the growth and spatial distribution of ICT adoption at the national and regional levels.

Following previous work by Wu *et al.* (2015), in this study, product innovation refers to new product success, which is the capability of successfully developing new products with superior quality and in a speedy manner for launching new products into the market and gaining market share. Product innovation is treated as a binary variable in this study and is coded as 1 if a firm introduces new products during the last three years, and 0 otherwise.

Following the work of Parida and Örtqvist (2015, p. 279), ICT adoption in this study refers to the extent to which a firm strategically uses "a wide array of information and communication technologies for business purposes, ranging from basic to very sophisticated ways". The Enterprises Survey of World Bank identifies five types of ICT media, namely, phone and fax, e-mail, electronic data interexchange (EDI), online web/Internet-based system, and software such as enterprises resource planning (ERP) systems, SCM systems and customer relationship management (CRM) systems. This survey also collects information about whether or not the surveyed firms adopt these different types of ICT media for their external inter-organization relationships and transactions. The variable is coded as 1 if the firm uses the specified ICT medium assigned by the survey, and 0 otherwise. The extent of ICT adoption in business activities of firms is measured by the 5-point Likert-scale, with 0 indicating no use of ICT in the business activities and 4 denoting use of ICT all the time. We mainly focus on ICT application to five types of business activities, namely R&D activities or product enhancement, production and operation, sales and marketing, partner (including supplier) relations, and customer relations.

To examine the impact of ICT adoption on the new product success of firms, one has to control for several important variables. (1) Firm age is calculated by the number of years since the foundation year. (2) Firm size is measured by the natural log of total number of full-time employees. (3) We use a dummy variable to control R&D activities, with 1 indicating that a firm conducted R&D activities during the last three years and 0 otherwise. (4) The extent of firms' ICT adoption is largely affected by local provision of ICT infrastructure. We therefore calculate the local ICT access rate based on data from China City Statistic Yearbook. Local ICT access rate is measured by total subscribers of telephone, mobile phone, and Internet divided by total population in a city.

5. ICT Adoption and Product Innovation of China's Manufacturing Firms

To test our hypotheses concerning the ICT adoption in internal business activities and external relationships on product innovation of China's manufacturing firms, we conduct a set of logit regression analyses. The results are listed in Table 2. The values of VIF are all under 4, indicating that the multi-collinearity is not a serious problem in our study (Hair *et al.* 1995). Overall, the models correctly assess more than 75% of the cases, which suggests that the control and independent variables well explained the probability of product innovation of China's manufacturing firms. Model 1 includes all of the control variables, among which R&D activities and local ICT access exert a significantly positive influence on the probability of product innovation. These two variables are still significant and strong even after we incorporate the independent variables into the model. It shows that internal R&D investment and activities are of particular importance to firm innovation, as also shown by others such as Jha and Bose (2016). Besides, a higher ratio of local ICT access suggests a better provision of ICT infrastructure of the city, which encourages local firms to use ICT for innovation.

As shown in Model 2, ICT applications in product enhancement significantly increase the probability of product innovation ($\beta = 1.199$, $p < 0.05$), which is similar to the findings of Durmusoglu and Barczak (2011) and Kawakami *et al.* (2011, 2015), and ICT applications in customer relations also significantly contribute to product innovation ($\beta = 1.182$, $p < 0.05$). However, ICT adoptions in internal production and operation, sales and marketing, as well as external relationship with suppliers and contractors are demonstrated to be insignificant for firm innovation. It suggests that ICT applications to different activities of value creation and to relationships with different knowledge sources would produce different influences on firm innovation. All other things being equal, ICT media that are used for R&D activities or product enhancement will be more likely to promote innovation than they are used for production process as

Table 2. Regression results of ICT adoption on product innovation.

DV: Product Innovation of Firms	Model 1	Model 2	Model 3
Firm age	0.999	0.993	0.995
Firm size	1.000	1.000	1.000
R&D	9.726***	7.720***	7.622***
Local ICT access	2.647**	2.093*	1.685
ICT adoption for business tasks			
ICT adoption in product enhancement		1.198*	
ICT adoption in production and operation		1.060	
ICT adoption in sales and marketing		1.157	
ICT adoption in partner relations		0.980	
ICT adoption in customer relations		1.182*	
ICT media used for inter-organizational relationships			
Phone and fax			0.891
Email			2.511***
EDI			0.827
Online web-based systems			0.943
Software (e.g., ERP, SCM systems)			2.113***
Chi-square and probability	449.712***	537.896***	504.843***
Probability of correct prediction	75.6%	75.2%	75.0%
Observations	1632	1574	1572

Notes: * $p < 0.05$, ** $p < 0.01$, *** $p < 0.001$ (two-tailed).

well as sales and marketing. In a similar vein, ICT media used for customer relations will be more beneficial to product innovation than they are used for partner relations. Therefore, we find support for our hypotheses 1a and 2b, but reject hypotheses 1b, 1c, and 2a.

While it is understandable that ICT used for product enhancement or R&D activities is more effective than it is used for other activities of value creation on firm innovation, it is not very self-evident for the result that ICT in customer relations plays a more important role than it is used for other relations in enhancing the probability of firm innovation. One potential explanation is that knowledge from customers is more valuable than that from suppliers and other partners, because customers can provide direct market-related information and knowledge, and sometimes even provide technology-related knowledge that is beneficial for the firm innovation (Nambisan and Baron, 2009). Therefore, ICT media enable firms to break geographical limitations to keep a frequent, timely, and close connection with their customers to foster the innovation performance of firms. Instead, as the customer of their suppliers, firms may find that ICT used for the supplier relations benefits more to their suppliers than from them. This difference impels us to explore the kinds of ICT media used for inter-firm relationships and whether or not these applications produce positive influences on innovation.

Model 3 shows the impact of different ICT media used for inter-firm relationships and transactions on product innovation of firms. It turns out that among the five types of ICT media identified by this study, only e-mail and software have a significantly positive influence on the product innovation. Other ICT media, such as phone and fax, EDI and online web-based systems are not significant. It indicates that not all ICT media used for inter-firm relationships exert the same influence on firm innovation. It is interesting to note that e-mail used for inter-firm relationship promotes product innovation, but phone and fax fail to do so. It implies that communication via the presence of text rather than voice may be more direct and effective for knowledge and information exchange.

By further probing into the database, we find that sample firms do not show a convergence in the use of ICT media, except for phone and fax that are adopted by almost all of surveyed firms (98%) for inter-organizational relationships and transactions (Table 3). About 79.6% and 69.1% of

Table 3. Types of ICT media used for inter-organizational relationships and transactions.

	Percent of Firms (%)
Phone and Fax	98.40
E-mail	79.58
Online web-based systems (Internet-based)	69.14
Software, such as ERP, SCM and CRM systems	47.58
EDI	37.96

Data source: Calculated from Enterprises Survey of World Bank, 2012.

surveyed firms report that they have used e-mail and online Internet-based systems for the same purpose, respectively. Only 47.6% of sampled firms report a use of software for external relationships and the number is even lower when it comes to the use of EDI (38%). It shows that the simple and economic ICT media without much financial investment are acceptable for a majority of China's manufacturing firms, but the popular ICT media such as phone and fax does not necessarily lead to an effective knowledge exchange and a better performance of innovation.

6. Discussion and Conclusion

The rapid growth of ICT in the current era has attracted much scholarly attention to the impact of ICT adoption on firm innovation. However, whether or not and how ICT adoption exerts influence on firm innovation in emerging countries, especially in China, still remains somewhat unexplored. The purpose of the study in this chapter is to examine the growth and spatial distribution of the ICT adoption in China and, more importantly, to investigate a long-time neglected role played by ICT applications to both internal business activities and external inter-firm relationships, on the innovation of Chinese manufacturing firms. This investigation generates several interesting findings.

First of all, it is found that the growth of China's ICT adoption is with an extreme spatial unevenness. Beijing, Shanghai, Zhejiang, and Guangdong outperform others by a large margin in terms of the use of telephone and Internet. Second, ICT adoption by firms in China progressed through a process of simply using computer and LAN within the functional department to a more sophisticated application of integrated management software and WAN in the whole organization during the last four decades. Third, a spatial autocorrelation analysis finds that spatial interdependence in terms of innovation is not very strong in China and innovative activities only agglomerated in a few of regions. Fourth, ICT application to internal product enhancement is positively associated with product innovation of firms. However, ICT used for production and operation as well as sales and marketing does not produce a significant influence on product innovation. Fifth, ICT used for maintaining external relations with customers, other than partners (suppliers and contractors) significantly increase the probability of product innovation. Sixth, phone and fax as well as email are the most popular ICT media adopted by Chinese firms for external linkages and connections, but the former fail to promote product innovation of firms. The use of email and software such as CRM and SCM for external linkages and communication significantly and positively affects product innovation. Finally, a higher level of region-level provision of ICT infrastructure leads to product innovation by fostering the ICT adoption by firms.

Overall, our study lends support to a positive relationship between ICT adoption and product innovation of firms in China, but argues that ICT applications to different fields would produce different influences on firm innovation. Moreover, existing research on ICT adoption is mainly based on SME observations which claim that ICT adoption may have a more important influence on the performance of SMEs than that of larger sized enterprises (Díaz-Chao *et al.* 2015). However, our study reveals that both firm size and firm age do not have significant effects in terms of product innovation. This shows that both SMEs and larger-sized enterprises benefit from ICT adoption in China, which is going through a significant transformation from a manufacturing-based economy to an innovation-based economy.

6.1. *Theoretical implications*

Our study has the following theoretical implications. First, the findings of our research cast doubt over the importance of geography in knowledge exchange and innovation. Whereas geographical proximity facilitates not only production linkages but also knowledge circulation among co-located firms, especially tacit knowledge that is believed to be shared only by face-to-face interactions, our research demonstrates that communications via ICT media with their customers can also speed up knowledge flows for a better innovation performance. In this regard, Kawakami *et al.* (2015) and Durmusoglu and Kawakami (2021) have shown that ICT use, which includes use of CRM software, enhances innovation. This study goes one step further to specifically examine the direct effect of CRM use on product innovation. It is argued that ICT provides a possibility to share tacit knowledge across geographical distances and hence cripple the importance of geography in firm innovation (Lazoi *et al.* 2011). Although the role of geography cannot be blindly overblown, the issue of whether or not ICT use, by enabling stronger ties to non-cluster partners can weaken or even replace the functions of industrial cluster, needs more empirical investigation (Steinfield and Scupola, 2008).

Second, this study provides a new perspective to the studies of firm's knowledge management, since ICT could serve as an effective knowledge management tool for knowledge sharing, flows, application, and creation within and among firms. More importantly, our study suggests that knowledge sourcing from customers is much more valuable than that from suppliers. This finding is not surprising given that a majority of manufacturing firms in China are market-oriented rather than technology-driven due to the huge domestic market demand. It also contributes to the debate over the role of externally heterogeneous knowledge sources in firm innovation (Zeng *et al.* 2010). At the global level, by establishing a global virtual space, ICT also can function as a global pipeline in parallel with international trade fair and transnational community to bridge international knowledge and local practices together for innovation (Bathelt and Li 2014; Daim *et al.* 2012). This appears extremely important for firms with a limited capability of internationalization or establishing a global pipeline for upgrading and innovation in developing countries, such as China.

In terms of limitations, our data did not allow us to distinguish between a firm that introduced many new products vs. only one new product. Hence, future research might use more accurate data to better explore the impact of ICT use on product innovation of Chinese firms.

6.2. *Managerial suggestions*

Our study has several managerial implications regarding ICT adoption by firms. First, the provision of ICT infrastructure may be quite uneven across the emerging economies. Therefore, local ICT infrastructure should be considered as a significant factor affecting the location of new branches (Gerguri-Rashiti *et al.* 2017).

Second, it is worth noting that ICT adoption and innovation are not well developed in some regions (see Figures 2 and 5). As for firms in regions with low level of ICT adoption and high level of patent activities,

R&D activities may be the main source of product innovation. By contrast, the most suitable strategies should be discussed for those firms in areas with a high level of ICT adoption and a low level of innovation. ICT allows new possibilities for the flow of knowledge and information, favoring the learning processes needed for product innovation. What is more, as for firms in regions with both low level of ICT access and patent activities (e.g., those in Tibet and Qinghai with poor location conditions in China), they might actively seek external support to obtain more ICT investment and complement their own knowledge with external knowledge sources.

Third, our findings also suggest that firms should give a high priority to ICT adoption and develop an ICT strategy to facilitate knowledge sharing within and beyond the boundary of firms, regardless of innovative capacity of firms. Age increase and scale expansion of firms do not necessarily induce innovation. Innovation is output which requires dedicated input. Managers in both SMEs and larger-sized enterprises need to recognize the importance of ICT adoption on innovation, despite the high cost of ICT adoption especially in large-sized enterprises. Finally, ICT adoption in production and operation or sales and marketing are insignificant to product innovation, but that in product enhancement and customer relations are positive.

References

Alam, S. S. and Noor, M. K. M. (2009). ICT adoption in small and medium enterprises: An empirical evidence of service sectors in Malaysia, *International Journal of Business and Management*, 4(2), 112–125.

Amit, R. and Zott, C. (2001). Value creation in e-business, *Strategic Management Journal*, 22(6–7), 493–520.

Atkinson, R. D. (2014). ICT innovation policy in China: A review. The Information Technology & Innovation Foundation. http://www2.itif.org/2014-china-ict.pdf.

Barczak, G., Hultink, E. J., and Sultan, F. (2008). Antecedents and consequences of information technology usage in NPD: A comparison of Dutch and US companies, *Journal of Product Innovation Management*, 25(6), 620–631.

Bathelt, H. and Li, P.-F. (2014). Global cluster networks-foreign direct investment flows from Canada to China, *Journal of Economic Geography*, 45–71.

Beijing CCID Publishing, Media Co., L. (2011). White Papers of the ICT adpotion of firms.

Bertazzon, S. (2003). Spatial and temporal autocorrelation in innovation/ diffusion analysis, *Lecture Notes in Computer Science*, 2669, 23–32.

Bertschek, I., Cerquera, D., and Klein, G. J. (2013). More bits — More bucks? Measuring the impact of broadband Internet on firm performance, *Information Economics and Policy*, 25(3), 190–203.

Brynjolfsson, E. and Hitt, L. M. (2003). Computing productivity: Firm-level evidence, *The Review of Economics and Statistics*, 85(4), 793–808.

Carbonara, N. (2005). Information and communication technology and geographical clusters: Opportunities and spread, *Technovation*, 25(3), 213–222.

Chung, S. and Kim, G. M. (2003). Performance effects of partnership between manufacturers and suppliers for new product development: The supplier's standpoint, *Research Policy*, 32(4), 587–603.

Cornell University, INSEAD, WIPO (2016). *The Global Innovation Index 2016: Winning with Global Innovation*, Ithaca, Fontainebleau, and Geneva.

Cornell University, INSEAD, and WIPO (2020). *The Global Innovation Index 2020: Who Will Finance Innovation?* Ithaca, Fontainebleau, and Geneva.

Daim, T. U., Ha, A., Reutiman, S. *et al.* (2012). Exploring the communication breakdown in global virtual teams, *International Journal of Project Management*, 30, 199–212.

Díaz-Chao, Á., Sainz-González, J., and Torrent-Sellens, J. (2015). ICT, innovation, and firm productivity: New evidence from small local firms, *Journal of Business Research*, 68(7), 1439–1444.

Dong, J. Q. and Netten, J. (2017). Information technology and external search in the open innovation age: New findings from Germany, *Technological Forecasting and Social Change*, 120, 223–231.

Dubiel, A., Brexendorf, T. O., and Glöckner, S. (2014). Keeping up with the Virtual Voice of the Customer — Social Media Applications in Product Innovation. In *Open Innovation*, eds. C. H. Noble, S. S. Durmusoglu and A. Griffin). https://doi.org/10.1002/9781118947166.ch3.

Durmusoglu, S. S. and Barczak, G. (2011). The use of information technology tools in new product development phases: Analysis of effects on new product innovativeness, quality, and market performance, *Industrial Marketing Management*, 40(2), 321–330.

Durmusoglu, S. S. and Kawakami, T. (2021). Information technology tools in new product development: The effects of stage-specific use frequency on performance, *Industrial Marketing Management*, 93, 250–258.

Fagerberg, J. (2005). Innovation: A guide to the literature. In *The Oxford Handbook of Innovation*, eds. J. Fagerberg, C. D. Mowery, R. R. Nelson, pp. 1–26. New York: Oxford University Press.

Fagerberg, J., Mowery, C. D., and Nelson, R. R. (Eds.) 2005. *The Oxford Handbook of Innovation*, Oxford: Oxford University Press.

Fariselli, P., Oughton, C., Picory, C., and Sugden, R. (1999). Electronic commerce and the future for SMEs in a global market-place: Networking and public policies, *Small Business Economics*, 12(3), 261–275.

Fu, X., Peitrobelli, C., and Soete, L. (2010). *The Role of Foreign Technology and Indigenous Innovation in Emerging Economies: Technological Change and Catching Up*, Washington D.C.: Inter-American Development Bank.

Gallego, J. M., Gutiérrez, L. H., and Lee, S. H. (2015). A firm-level analysis of ICT adoption in an emerging economy: Evidence from the Colombian manufacturing industries, *Industrial and Corporate Change*, 24(1), 191–221.

Gerguri-Rashiti, S., Ramadani, V., Abazi-Alili, H., Dana, L.-P., and Ratten, V. (2017). ICT, innovation and firm performance: The transition economies context, *Thunderbird International Business Review*, 59(1), 93–102.

Hair, J. F. Jr., Anderson, R. E., Tatham, R. L., and Black, W. C. (1995). *Multivariate Data Analysis*, 3rd ed. New York: Macmillan.

Hall, B. H., Lotti, F., and Mairesse, J. (2013). Evidence on the impact of R&D and ICT investments on innovation and productivity in Italian firms, *Economics of Innovation and New Technology*, 22(3), 300–328.

Hempell, T., Leeuwen, G. V., Wiel, H. V. D. (2004). ICT, innovation and business performance in services: Evidence for Germany and the Netherlands: ZEW — Centre for European Economic Research Discussion Paper.

Higón, D. A. (2012). The impact of ICT on innovation activities: Evidence for UK SMEs, *International Small Business Journal*, 30(6), 684–699.

Jha, A. K. and Bose, I. (2016). Innovation in IT firms: An investigation of intramural and extramural R&D activities and their impact, *Information & Management*, 53(4), 409–421.

Kawakami, T., Barczak, G., and Durmusoglu, S. S. (2015). Information technology tools in new product development: The impact of complementary resources, *Journal of Product Innovation Management*, 32(4), 622–635.

Kawakami, T., Durmusoglu, S. S., and Barczak, G. (2011). Factors influencing Information Technology usage for new product development: The case of Japanese companies, *Journal of Product Innovation Management*, 28(6), 833–847.

Kossaï, M. and Piget, P. (2014). Adoption of information and communication technology and firm profitability: Empirical evidence from Tunisian SMEs, *The Journal of High Technology Management Research*, 25(1), 9–20.

Kraemer, K. L., Gibbs, J., and Dedrick, J. (2005). Impacts of globalization on E-commerce use and firm performance: A cross-country investigation, *Information Society*, 21(5), 323–340.

Lazoi, M., Ceci, F., Corallo, A., and Secundo, G. (2011). Collaboration in an amrospace SMEs cluster: Innovation and ICT dynamics, *International Journal of Innovation and Technology Management*, 8(3), 393–414.

Lopez-Nicolas, C. and Soto-Acosta, P. (2010). Analyzing ICT adoption and use effects on knowledge creation: An empirical investigation in SMEs, *International Journal of Information Management*, 30(6), 521–528.

Melecky, L. (2015). Spatial autocorrelation method for local analysis of the EU, *Procedia Economics and Finance*, 23, 1102–1109.

Meng, Q. and Li, M. (2002). New economy and ICT development in China, *Information Economics and Policy*, 14, 275–295.

Molla, A. and Heeks, R. (2007). Exploring e-commerce benefits for businesses in a developing country, *Information Society*, 23(2), 95–108.

Morikawa, M. (2004). Information technology and the performance of Japanese SMEs, *Small Business Economics*, 23(3), 171–177.

Mustaffa, S. and Beaumont, N. (2004). The effect of electronic commerce on small Australian enterprises, *Technovation*, 24(2), 85–95.

Nambisan, S. and Baron, R. A. (2009). Virtual customer environments: Testing a Model of voluntary participation in value co-creation activities, *Journal of Product Innovation Management*, 26(4), 388–406.

NBSC (2012). *China City Statistical Yearbook 2012.* Beijing: China Statistical Press.

Nieto, M. J. and Santamaría, L. (2007). The importance of diverse collaborative networks for the novelty of product innovation, *Technovation*, 27(6–7), 367–377.

Ollo-López, A. and Aramendía-Muneta, M. E. (2012). ICT impact on competitiveness, innovation and environment, *Telematics and Informatics*, 29(2), 204–210.

Parida, V. and Örtqvist, D. (2015). Interactive effects of network capability, ICT capability, and financial slack on technology-based small firm innovation performance, *Journal of Small Business Management*, 53, 278–298.

Reeson, A. and Rudd, L. (2016). ICT activity, innovation and productivity: An analysis of data from Australian businesses, *Economic Papers*, 35(3), 245–255.

Sørensen, C. and Snis, U. (2001). Innovation through knowledge codification, *Journal of Information and Technology*, 16, 83–97.

Sambamurthy, V. and Subramani, M. (2005). Special issue on information technologies and knowledge management, *MIS Quarterly*, 29(1), 1–7.

Skoko, H., Ceric, A., and Huang, C.-Y. (2008). ICT adoption model of Chinese SMEs. Online at http://mpra.ub.uni-muenchen.de/11540/.

Steinfield, C. and Scupola, A. (2008). Understanding the role of ICT networks in a biotechnology cluster: An exploratory study of Medicon valley, *The Information Society*, 24(5), 319–333.

Steinfield, C., Scupola, A., and López-Nicolás, C. (2010). Social capital, ICT use and company performance: Findings from the Medicon Valley Biotech Cluster, *Technological Forecasting and Social Change*, 77(7), 1156–1166.

Sun, Z., Hou, J., and Li, J. (2017). The multifaceted role of information and communication technology in innovation: Evidence from Chinese manufacturing firms, *Asian Journal of Technology Innovation*, 25(1), 168–183.

Tang, M. and Hussler, C. (2011). Betting on indigenous innovation or relying on FDI: The Chinese strategy for catching-up, *Technology in Society*, 33(1–2), 23–35.

Thompson, E. R. (2002). Clustering of foreign direct investment and enhanced technology transfer: Evidence from Hong Kong garment firms in China, *World Development*, 30(5), 873–889.

Tsai, K.-H. (2009). Collaborative networks and product innovation performance: Toward a contingency perspective, *Research Policy*, 38(5), 765–778.

Vaccaro, A., Parente, R., and Veloso, F. M. (2010). Knowledge management tools, inter-organizational relationships, innovation and firm performance, *Technological Forecasting and Social Change*, 77(7), 1076–1089.

Venkatraman, N. and Henderson, J. C. (1998). Real strategies for virtual organizing, *Sloan Management Review*, 40(1), 33–48.

Vilaseca-Requena, J., Torrent-Sellens, J., and Jiménez-Zarco, A. I. (2007). ICT use in marketing as innovation success factor: Enhancing cooperation in new product development processes, *European Journal of Innovation Management*, 10(2), 268–288.

Vu, K. M. (2011). ICT as a source of economic growth in the information age: Empirical evidence from the 1996–2005 period, *Telecommunications Policy*, 35(4), 357–372.

Wang, C. C. and Lin, G. C. S. (2010). Industrial clustering and technological innovation in China: New evidence from the ICT industry in Shenzhen, *Environment and Planning A*, 42, 1987–2010.

Wang, C. C. and Lin, G. C. S. (2013). Dynamics of innovation in a globalizing China: Regional environment, inter-firm relations and firm attributes, *Journal of Economic Geography*, 13(3), 397–418.

Warner, E. (2015). Patenting and innovation in China: Incentives, policy, and outcomes. Pardee RAND Graduate, 2015.

Wasko, M. M. and Faraj, S. (2005). Why should I share? Examining social capital and knowledge contribution in electronic networks of practice, *MIS Quarterly*, 29(1), 35–57.

World Economic Forum, Cornell University, INSEAD (2016). The Global Information Technology Report 2016. Geneva: World Economic Forum.

Wu, F., Mahajan, V., and Balasubramanian, S. (2003). An analysis of e-business adoption and its impact on business performance, *Journal of the Academy of Marketing Science*, 31(4), 425–447.

Wu, A., Wang, C. C., and Li, S. (2015). Geographical knowledge search, internal R&D intensity and product innovation of clustering firms in Zhejiang, China, *Papers in Regional Science*, 94(3), 553–572.

Wu, X. and Zhang, W. (2010). Seizing the opportunity of paradigm shifts: Catching-up of Chinese ICT firms, *International Journal of Innovation Management*, 14(1), 57–91.

Xie, X. (2000). On the enterprise informationization and its environment optimization of China, *Journal of Peking University*, 37(5), 21–29.

Young, S. and Lan, P. (2010). Technology transfer to China through foreign direct investment, *Regional Studies*, 31, 669–679.

Zeng, S. X., Xie, X. M., and Tam, C. M. (2010). Relationship between cooperation networks and innovation performance of SMEs, *Technovation*, 30(3), 181–194.

Zhou, Q. N., Gao, P., and Chimhowu, A. (2019). ICTs in the transformation of rural enterprises in China: A multi-layer perspective, *Technological Forecasting and Social Change*, 145, 12–23.

Open-Source Software Platform Innovation in China: Past, Present, and the Future

Sai Lan, Junsong Chen, and Kun Liu

1. Open-Source Software Ecosystem

Since its inception over two decades ago, the open-source software (OSS) movement has evolved into a global open innovation ecosystem (Adner and Kapoor 2015; Bogers *et al.* 2017), which continues to generate profoundly impactful innovations that have shaped the landscape in cloud computing, block chain, data management, and many other domains in the IT industries. More importantly, many of the OSS are platforms, defined as technological infrastructures provide foundational building blocks upon which other firms can develop complementary goods and services (Fitzgerald 2006; Gawer 2014; O'Mahony and Karp 2020). These open platforms have become the keystones of large-scale platform ecosystems with numerous complementors, which enable value co-creation and sharing (Adner 2017; Boudreau 2010).

The competitive advantages of such open-source platform ecosystems include, but are not limited to the following: network effects, ease of access, wide adoption, standard setting, value co-creation, and profit sharing. These advantages attracted many established companies, such as IBM and Google, to join the OSS ecosystem. These companies played crucial leadership roles in fostering the growth of the OSS ecosystem into a mainstream model of innovation and competition. In recent years, Chinese firms such as Alibaba, Baidu, and Huawei also joined the OSS ecosystem, and became important contributors to the global OSS community. In this chapter, we will examine some of the most prominent OSS platforms sponsored by Chinese firms, such as the Harmony OS from Huawei.

1.1. *History of OSS ecosystem*

OSS used to be developed primarily by volunteers who are also users of the software themselves, in a loosely connected developer community, and distributed free of charge. The Linux operating system and Apache web server are perhaps the most prominent examples of OSS projects. Together they have taken a dominant share of the web server market. OSS represents a major departure from proprietary software in almost all major aspects, including input, output, development process, and value proposition (Fitzgerald 2006).

The proprietary software development process is similar to traditional product development. It involves development stages such as planning, requirement analysis, design, implementation, and testing. These tasks are typically carried out within the boundary of a single firm. The firm provides all the resources for the development, controls the process, and appropriates all the profits from the final product. In contrast, OSS projects are developed beyond the confines of any single firm. They are typically initiated by individual developers or small groups of developers who are also users of the software. The planning and design phases are often simplified due to the generalized nature of the problems these OSS projects attempt to address. Few resources are needed as the input to the OSS development process because OSS relies on volunteer contributions. The coordination of the development process is usually achieved through online development forums and mailing lists. Finally, the output is freely available to everyone.

Beyond the differences in the development process, the most fundamental distinction between open source and proprietary software is the value proposition. While proprietary software firms can appropriate all the rents generated by their products, no party is supposed to directly profit from OSS. As a public good, OSS is supposed to be free to the masses and not to generate private profits for those who contributed to its development. On the other hand, public firms are under pressure to create value for their shareholders. This creates a seemingly paradoxical situation: profit-oriented firms making investments in non-profit-generating OSS development. Prior empirical studies on OSS have examined the motivations of individual developers who contribute their software development efforts for free (Krishnamurthy *et al.* 2014; Roberts *et al.* 2006) or factors affecting the outcome of OSS development processes (Curto-Millet and Shaikh 2017; Setia *et al.* 2020; Shah, 2006). However, little attention has been given to the case of firm sponsorship of OSS, or its performance implications. Among the research studies that did examine firm involvement in OSS, most adopted a case study approach (West and Gallagher 2006) and were concerned with small, entrepreneurial firms adopting OSS-based business models (Colombo *et al.* 2014; O'Mahony and Bechky 2008; Stam and Elfring 2008). Nevertheless, based on the history of OSS ecosystems, sponsorship by large, established firms, such as IBM, HP, and SUN, is crucial for the commercial success of OSS ecosystem today. This chapter attempts to explain this seemingly paradoxical phenomenon of public firm sponsorship of OSS through the theoretical lens of open innovation and knowledge-based perspectives.

1.1.1. *Evolution of the OSS ecosystem*

Taking a longitudinal view of the OSS literature, we may identify two distinct phases of OSS research, which also correspond with the evolution of the open-source movement. First, the inward-looking phase (OSS 1.0), in which the newly emerging OSS movement phenomenon is at center stage. Second, the outward-looking phase (OSS 2.0) (Fitzgerald 2006), in which the relationships between OSS and business firms captured academic attention and became the new research focus.

1.1.2. *OSS 1.0*

In the early days of the OSS movement, much attention has been devoted to the interpretation of the open-source phenomenon. The common goal of these early research studies was to reconcile the seemingly unorthodox approach of software development with the traditional economic paradigm. Specifically, the OSS movement presents research challenges in the following two interrelated aspects: (1) individual incentives — can OSS really be understood as "gift economies" (Bergquist and Ljungberg 2001; Krishnamurthy *et al.* 2014)? How does it reconcile with the self-interest-seeking behavioral assumptions of the economics discipline? (2) innovation model — is this self-managed innovation model a sustainable new innovation model? How to reconcile this model with the traditional innovation processes driven by protection of intellectual property rights, such as patents, copyrights, and trademarks (Lerner and Tirole 2001)? These concerns are valid and resolving them will enhance the understanding of the OSS phenomenon itself.

Researchers conducted mostly case studies and surveys in order to answer the first set of questions. While the gift economy explanation may have certain merits judging by the special norms and ideology within the open-source community (Daniel *et al.* 2018; Stewart and Gosain 2006), individual participants are more likely driven by user value (Franke and von Hippel 2003; Lakhani and von Hippel 2003), reputation and status (Zeitlyn 2003), or career advancement concerns (Lerner and Tirole 2002). Other researchers found these individual motives to be interrelated in complex ways, which could impact the level of participation and contribution (Roberts *et al.* 2006). Overall, the motivations of OSS developers can indeed be reconciled with the conventional individual behavioral assumptions in business and economics.

The second set of questions is more intriguing to firms trying to understand the viability as well as sustainability of OSS as a new innovation model (Curto-Millet and Shaikh 2017; Dalle and Jullien 2003; Osterloh and Rota 2007). The tremendous potential of the open-source innovation model could be invigorating for some industry players and threatening for others. Proprietary software giant Microsoft assessed OSS such as the Linux operating system, and concluded that this threat is real and could turn into a horror story for its monopoly position in the market if unchecked.[1] This explained why Microsoft took on an aggressive role from the beginning of the open-source movement, to launch numerous lawsuits aimed at undermining the legitimacy of Linux,[2] and the OSS innovation model in general.

On the theory building side, academics have attempted to define this new innovation model as a "private-collective" innovation model (von Hippel and von Krogh 2003), with private efforts from user-innovators amounting to collective innovation that benefits the society at large. At the same time, the open-source innovation model was recognized as a community-based knowledge creation model, distinct from firm-based commercial software development model. Empirically, substantial research efforts have been devoted to in-depth examination of the determinants of successful OSS development processes. Observations have been made about contributor behavior (David and Rullani 2008; Lindberg *et al.* 2016), impact of social network structure (Grewal *et al.* 2006; Hahn *et al.* 2008), knowledge sharing (Kuk 2006), and modularity of code structure (MacCormack *et al.* 2006), among other factors. Another important area of the open-source innovation process is its governance (Di Tullio and Staples 2013). Important determinants related to governance include license choices (Lerner and Tirole 2005), conceptions of authority (O'Mahony and Ferraro 2007), and control mechanisms (Shah 2006).

In summary, the research questions in the OSS 1.0 phase mostly aimed at making sense of the new phenomenon of OSS movement, connecting it to conventional economics reasoning, and examining the specific innovation processes. In other words, the focus is inside the open-source innovation model. Therefore, research in this stage is considered inward-looking.

1.1.3. *OSS 2.0*

In the OSS 1.0 phase, important research questions regarding the relationship between OSS and its external environments have been to a large extent neglected. For example, few research studies have examined the

---

[1] http://en.wikipedia.org/wiki/Halloween_Documents.

[2] http://money.cnn.com/magazines/fortune/fortune_archive/2007/05/28/100033867/index.htm.

competitive implications of OSS in high-tech industries. The development of the industry is leading to the call for more outward-looking research studies of the OSS phenomenon, with a focus on its competitive impacts. For instance, a survey among Norwegian software companies confirmed that close to 50% of the software industry integrated OSS into their solutions, and more than 30% of the firms surveyed have more than 40% of their incomes from products related to OSS (Hauge *et al.* 2008).

The open-source literature has witnessed a boom of research studies looking beyond the open-source community into its social impacts on business firm competition as well as government environments (Alexy *et al.* 2018; Simon 2005). This is a major shift from the OSS 1.0 stage, representing a more outward-looking research focus. Increasingly, the interactions between firms and the OSS communities are being studied. Further, more diverse methodologies have been used as well, including case study, survey, archival data, and simulations. This new stage of the OSS research has been labeled "OSS 2.0" (Fitzgerald 2006), to distinguish it from the previously inward-looking focus in the earlier stage of open-source research.

In fact, research related to the interrelationship between OSS and firm involvement dates back to the beginning of the open-source movement. Early work linking OSS to business strategy proposed that OSS is ideal for platform-based strategies, mainly because OSS developers have the most experiences in the infrastructure/back-end software space (Behlendorf 1999). In other words, this work acknowledged: (1) the path-dependent nature of knowledge creation in open-source movement, and (2) both strengths and weaknesses exist for OSS-based business strategies. Early academic research in OSS also noticed the phenomenon of corporate resource allocation to foster open-source activities, thus putting the research question about the motives for corporate sponsorship of OSS on the future research agenda (Lerner and Tirole 2001). This literature stream on firm involvement in OSS witnessed a takeoff soon afterwards.

Similar to the research questions in OSS 1.0 stage, the most important research areas in the OSS 2.0 era also have to do with two interrelated questions regarding the motives for participation and process issues, although this time the questions are asked at the firm level: (1) What are the key motives for companies to sponsor OSS? (2) How do companies leverage OSS in their business strategies to achieve competitive advantage? A quick review of the extant OSS literature may help us answer these two questions.

1.1.3.1. Firm motives in OSS 2.0

For the first question regarding firms' motives in sponsoring OSS, researchers proposed that both firms and the individual open-source programmers within them can benefit from contributing to the open-source community. The firm-employed open-source developers can benefit from skill improvement, pleasure away from routine work, and better career opportunities. Firms can benefit from proprietary expertise that is complementary to the OSS, and also from learning effects and good public relations (Lerner *et al.* 2006). Empirical support for this complementary expertise motive has been found (Fosfuri *et al.* 2008), in which a firm's expertise is measured by patents and trademarks. In addition, open-source communities have been recognized as complementary assets for business firms to leverage during their innovation processes (Dahlander and Magnusson 2008; O'Mahony and Karp 2020; Stam 2009).

Based on a comparison between firm and individual motives in open-source participation, a systematic framework suggests that firms may be motivated by: (1) economic factors such as profiting from complementary software-related services and products, (2) social factors such as the norms and expectations for firms utilizing OSS to contribute back to the open-source community, and (3) technological factors such as the reduction in R&D costs and enhancement of software quality (Fitzgerald 2006). A survey of 146 Italian OSS vendors found that a minority of firms (19%) were altruistically motivated (e.g., following norms of the open-source community), the rest of them are either entirely motivated by profit concerns (34%), or motivated by a mixture of profit and other concerns (Bonaccorsi and Rossi 2006). Finally, the innovation-enhancing potential of OSS has been noted in both theoretical and empirical papers. The OSS-based innovation model is viewed as a form of user innovation that could contribute to the firm competitiveness (Stuermer *et al.* 2009; Wen *et al.* 2016). The collaborative development model and shared property rights associated with OSS have also made it a quintessential example of open innovation. There are four types of open-source strategies as solutions to meet the challenges of open innovation: (1) pooled R&D — firms collaborate in R&D of projects like Linux and Firefox, while exploiting the collective innovation outcome to sell related products, (2) spinouts — firms transfer internal development projects to externally visible open-source projects (such as IBM's Eclipse), which may generate demands for the firms' products and/or services, (3) selling complements — firms can sell products/services complementary to the OSS, as in the case of Red Hat providing value-added services to its Linux, and (4) donated complements — firms release the OSS projects to seek free labor for valuable complements in the form of user generated innovations, such as PC game "Mods" (West and Gallagher 2006).

1.1.3.2. Firm competitive strategies in OSS 2.0

For the second question regarding OSS-based competitive strategy, some case studies have examined companies such as Apple, IBM, and Sun Microsystems. These case studies found that successful platforms typically require hybrid strategies, combing proprietary, and open-source components (Lerner and Schankerman 2010; West 2003). The benefits of hybrid strategies are also corroborated by other studies (Bonaccorsi *et al.* 2006). Start-up companies may represent the most innovative and dynamic members of the technology economy. Researchers have examined how effective these new ventures were able to leverage the open-source-based business strategies in market entry and competition (Dahlander 2007; Stam and Elfring 2008; Wen *et al.* 2016). In particular, the availability of OSS project repositories like SourceForge.net and Github enabled large-scale quantitative studies to examine corporate contributions to OSS projects, leading to the findings of a number of determinants for effective firm involvement in open-source sponsorship (Setia *et al.* 2020).

Overall, the OSS 2.0 phase research studies turned their attentions outside the open-source movement itself into the business environment, acknowledging the important role played by OSS in business strategies of firms, particularly as complementary assets allowing firms to profit from their advantageous resource positions (Alexy *et al.* 2018; Fosfuri *et al.* 2008; Pisano 2006). On the other hand, researchers have also recognized both the strengths and the limitations of open-source-based strategies, such as the strength in platform strategies and the weakness in end-user applications (Behlendorf 1999; Fitzgerald 2006). These limitations lead to the "essential tension" between innovation adoption vs. profit appropriation (West 2003). Hence, hybrid business strategies are postulated as the best ways to leverage OSS (Bonaccorsi *et al.* 2006; West 2003).

Much has changed since the beginning of open-source movement a few decades ago. Over the years, OSS has transformed itself from a grassroots movement confined within software developer communities into a mainstream and commercially viable form of business model (Fitzgerald 2006). In the era of OSS 2.0, OSS has become increasingly leveraged by commercial firms in their business strategies. Contributions to OSS projects no longer come only from individual developers who volunteer their work, but more from for-profit companies.[3] In certain product markets such as embedded systems, OSS has been widely adopted by commercial firms (Henkel 2006). As a matter of fact, studies show that 40% of all OSS codes are contributed by corporate employed programmers (Lakhani and Wolf 2005). Further, 75% of Linux codes are written by paid software developers at major corporations.[4] The huge success of the OSS-based Android system in the smart phone market[5] serves as a good example of the popularity of OSS in the business world.

Although the main competitive advantage of OSS seems to be in its low cost, an independent survey by Yankee Group reveals no clear-cut advantage in terms of Total Cost of Ownership (TCO) when comparing mainstream Linux systems (e.g., Red Hat) with Windows Server software (DiDio 2005). In fact, many corporations are embracing OSS such as Linux not for low-cost concerns, but for its openness and innovation potentials. For example, Oracle is an active contributor to Linux development. As a widely adopted open-source platform, Linux enables Oracle to tweak the operating system kernel in order to enhance the performance and functionalities of its cash-cow database product.[6] This is unlikely

---

[3] http://news.cnet.com/8301-13846_3-10315545-62.html.
[4] http://apcmag.com/linux-now-75-corporate.htm.
[5] http://news.cnet.com/8301-1035_3-20015799-94.html.
[6] http://www.oracle.com/us/technologies/linux/026042.htm.

accomplished with closed source operating systems like Windows. Another good example would be Apple, whose proprietary operating system has been plagued with instability problems,[7] and consequently suffered from loss of market shares for a long time. Apple achieved a dramatic comeback in the PC market around year 2000[8] with the launch of Mac OS X, which signaled a major strategic change in which Apple abandoned their crash-prone proprietary operating system and rebuilt their PC operating system on top of OSS. As a result, the stability of Mac OS was greatly improved. In a sense, OSS contributed to Apple regaining their PC market share. This critical strategic decision to embrace OSS laid the foundation for Apple's later spectacular expansion into its iPod/iPhone/iPad businesses. The list goes on. Based on a study about how firms deal with the tradeoff between open-source and proprietary software, researchers found that a "comingled code" approach — hybrid strategies combining open-source and proprietary software to exploit their complementarities — is the common pattern for businesses across countries (Lerner and Schankerman 2010).

Next, we conduct a review on the relationship between OSS and firm value creation, which may help to shed light on the corporate motives in embracing OSS and allow us to gain a deeper understanding of the value creation potentials of OSS.

1.2. *OSS and firm value creation*

1.2.1. *Innovation enhancing*

There have been some debates in the literature about the implications of OSS on firm innovation (Bonaccorsi and Rossi 2006). Despite some concerns that OSS is mostly imitation of proprietary software, the positive impacts of OSS on firm innovation seem to have gained more support. It has been argued that the collaborative nature of OSS development is particularly suitable for innovation (Raymond 1999). OSS projects are often tightly linked with firms' user communities (Daniel *et al.* 2018;

---

[7]http://whynotmac.net76.net/reason12.html.

[8]http://www.bspcn.com/2007/10/16/1997-2007-the-10-year-apple-comeback/.

Henkel 2009). They are not only open for user access but also open for user modification and contribution. It is also crucial that many of the OSS projects are highly modularized, horizontal platforms by nature (Fitzgerald 2006; O'Mahony and Karp 2020). These features facilitate the incorporation of new ideas into the OSS projects, and enhancing both the innovativeness and competitiveness of these software products (Dalle and Jullien 2003). In addition, customers may participate in the customization of the product and become more committed (Goldman and Gabriel 2005; von Hippel 2001), and open-source community developers can help to improve and support the software as well (Lakhani and von Hippel 2003; Lindberg *et al.* 2016). Hence, firm sponsorship of OSS projects could potentially stimulate knowledge exchange between internal and external developers and to enhance the firms' innovation capabilities through collaborative innovation activities (Baldwin and von Hippel 2011). Finally, OSS platforms allow firms with limited R&D budgets to focus on the technology niche on which their competitiveness depends. Many of the aforementioned innovation-enhancing benefits of OSS can be found in this quote from the VP of Systems and E-Commerce Engineering at Netflix[9]:

> We develop and apply great software technology to deliver a great streaming video experience. Our budget, measured in dollars, time, people, and energy, is limited and we must therefore focus our technology development efforts on that streaming video software that clearly differentiates Netflix and creates delight for our customers. These limits require that we stand on the shoulders of giants who have solved technology challenges shared in common by all companies that operate at Internet scale ... We do utilize some commercial software but there is often the alternative choice of utilizing OSS, preferably OSS that implements an open standard ... The great thing about a good open source project that solves a shared challenge is that it develops its own momentum and it is sustained for a long time by a virtuous cycle of continuous improvement ... By sharing our bug fixes and new features back out into the community, the community then in turn continues to improve upon bug fixes and new features that originated at Netflix and then we complete the cycle by bring those improvements back into Netflix.

---

[9]http://techblog.netflix.com/2010/12/why-we-use-and-contribute-to-open.html.

The innovation-enhancing effects of OSS is most closely related to the concept of open innovation, which is the reason that OSS development has been one of the most widely studied contexts in the open innovation literature.

1.2.2. *Signaling*

Public firms are concerned with shareholder value creation. The stock market value of a public firm depends to a large extent on the market perception of the value of its assets, among which a firm's knowledge endowments may be a key component (Grant 1996a; Liebeskind 1996). Thus, it is necessary for public firms to try to influence this market perception in its favor. However, knowledge assets are difficult for the market to evaluate due to information asymmetry. Furthermore, a thorough transfer of knowledge for the purpose of informing external stakeholders about firm value may potentially result in profit expropriation by imitators (Kogut and Zander 1992). Therefore, firms may choose to signal the value of their knowledge instead of bringing it to the market to recognize its value, in which signaling is defined as "conduct and observable attributes that alter the beliefs of, or convey information to, other individuals in the market about unobservable attributes and intentions" (Ndofor and Levitas 2004, p. 688).

OSS release could be used as the tool for signaling (Setia *et al.* 2020), resulting in at least two types of outcomes. First, in the case of firms making major investments in OSS, such as IBM and Sun Microsystems, effective signals can be sent to the market that create a *separating equilibrium* (Ndofor and Levitas 2004), indicating superior knowledge endowments related to this kind of collaborative innovation. Second, in the case of firms making tentative investments in OSS, such as Computer Associates,[10] a *pooling equilibrium* (Ndofor and Levitas 2004) may be achieved, with

---

[10]Computer Associates is a major enterprise software vendor, which open-sourced its Ingres database in 2004, but did not follow up with further open-source projects. See: https://www.eweek.com/database/ca-releases-open-source-windows-version-of-ingres-database.

less distinctive separation from other firms but favorable association with the innovation enhancing potential of open-source innovation model. Both of these types of signaling effects may positively influence the market perception of the value of the focal firm's knowledge assets. Therefore, a signaling effect could be a viable value creation mechanism adopted by public firms in sponsoring OSS.

1.2.3. *Competitive positioning*

Openness of the software may facilitate adoption because it can help to reduce the risks of adoption. First, openness facilitates modification and customization, which supports greater opportunity of learning and experimentation. Second, the open and participative development processes of OSS enable a smooth migration path, which helps to ensure backward and forward compatibility. Third, the low-cost nature of OSS reduces barriers to ownership, thus enhancing the network externality effect. Finally, the fact that OSS is not controlled by any single firm virtually eliminates the risk of technological lock-in. Even though OSS wins in adoption at the cost of direct profit appropriation (West 2003), indirect rents can be generated for the sponsoring firm through at least two mechanisms: (1) complementary assets and capabilities, and (2) increasing returns to adoption.

First, firms may profit from their complementary assets or capabilities (Teece 1986) for the OSS, which might include advantageous downstream asset positions in middleware, applications, hardware, and services (Pisano 2006). For example, the business models of the leading OSS firms, such as Red Hat Inc., is primarily based on selling support and service to their OSS products. Additionally, extant literature identified open-source communities as complementary assets for firms (Dahlander and Wallin 2006). Thus, firms may gain from support of the open-source communities in terms of development costs and user support.

Second, increasing returns to adoption is a common phenomenon in network industries such as telecommunication and software industries. The concept of increasing returns to adoption refers to the fact that the more a technology is adopted, the more improvement, or value its adopters get (Arthur 1989). This kind of increase in value may be found either in direct physical networks such as the telephone network, or indirectly through wider availability of products compatible to each other, also known as the hardware–software paradigm (Katz and Shapiro 1985). The drivers of this phenomenon include learning, network externalities (Teece 2006), and signaling effects (Schilling 1999). Hence, the increased returns to adoption tend to create a "virtuous cycle" for the adoption of OSS (Schilling 1999). As a result, firms may release OSS as a means to achieve dominant position in the market against their competitors. Later, they may exploit their advantageous positions in the market through exercise of market power or complementary assets. Economic value would therefore be created for these sponsor firms of OSS. See Table 1 for the details of firm value creation mechanisms with OSS.

Table 1.   OSS and firm value creation.

OSS Value Creation Mechanisms		Relevant Literature
Innovation enhancing	• Facilitates user innovation on modularized and open platforms. • Stimulates knowledge exchange across firm boundaries. • Enables smaller firms to focus on their technology niches instead of reinventing the wheel.	Lakhani and von Hippel (2003) Fitzgerald (2006) Daniel *et al.* (2018) O'Mahony and Karp (2020)
Signaling	• Alleviates the difficulties for the market to value firm knowledge assets caused by information asymmetry and knowledge transaction costs. • Achieves OSS-based market signaling through either separating equilibrium or pooling equilibrium.	Ndofor and Levitas (2004) Setia *et al.* (2020)
Competitive positioning	• Facilitates technology adoption by reducing the associated risks. • Leverages complementary assets as well as increasing returns to adoption to make profits.	West (2003) Teece (1986, 2006) Pisano (2006) Schilling (1999) Alexy *et al.* (2018)

1.2.4. *Challenges for firms in managing OSS value creation*

The open innovation and value creation model for public firms based on OSS and open-source communities is not without its risks and challenges. The fundamental issue here is that the individuals involved in these open-source communities are beyond the hierarchical control of the firm. In contrast to the closed innovation model, the diverse background of the participants, the decentralized innovation processes (Pitt *et al.* 2006), and the heterogeneous motives in this open-source innovation model together determine the benefits of innovative discovery, which also come with the costs of misaligned interests and divergent goals (Almirall and Casadesus-Masanell 2010). This misalignment increases the risks of firm investment in sponsoring these OSS projects (Dahlander *et al.* 2008; Daniel *et al.* 2018), which largely explains why there are substantial performance variances among public firm sponsorship events as evaluated by the stock market. Considering these challenges of managing the open- source-based innovation, this study proposes that only firms with strong knowledge capabilities may effectively leverage the knowledge resources within these open-source communities and fully benefit from the OSS-based innovation model. In fact, this knowledge- and capability-based perspective resonates with a number of extant open innovation literature in various contexts (Grand *et al.* 2004; Harison and Koski 2010). Next, we will explore these knowledge capabilities in the context of OSS sponsorship.

1.3. *OSS-based knowledge strategy*

Consistent with Zack's (1999) definition, this chapter defines *knowledge strategy* as the set of strategic choices a firm makes, in an effort to align its knowledge resources and capabilities with its business strategy, in order to achieve competitive advantage. Based on this definition, the sponsorship of OSS projects by public firms may be viewed as a manifestation of these firms' knowledge strategy. First, OSS represents a form of external knowledge, which can be utilized to complement and reshape the sponsoring firm's private knowledge base. Second, the choice of which OSS projects to sponsor is typically based on a firm's self-evaluation of its current knowledge base and the target knowledge resources and capabilities it intends to build up to. In other words, these are strategic choices aimed at filling a firm's knowledge gaps and transforming its knowledge base into a more desirable state. Third, OSS is not directly profit-generating. Thus, the sponsorship of OSS projects is not in itself a business strategy, at least not in a narrow sense. Lastly and most importantly, these firm initiatives in OSS sponsorship are planned rather than random efforts, aimed at aligning firms' knowledge resource base with their business strategies to improve firm performance. Even though some of these sponsored OSS projects may turn out to be casual experimentations with a new and fashionable idea, by and large most firms are making serious investments in these OSS initiatives in terms of both capital and human resources. For these public firms, such investments necessarily demand financial payoff. Thus, these OSS initiatives are ultimately profit motivated. The best way to achieve the profit goals of these sponsoring firms is to adapt their knowledge bases to achieve co-alignment with their business strategies. In this sense, we may best categorize these OSS sponsorship initiatives as knowledge strategy, based on the definition in this chapter.

Following prior research literature on the dimensions of knowledge strategy (Bierly and Chakrabarti 1996), OSS sponsorship as a knowledge strategy touches on almost all major dimensions including: (1) internal vs. external learning; (2) radical vs. incremental learning; (3) fast vs. slow learning; (4) depth and breadth of firm knowledge base. In addition, the unique nature of OSS production process presents a brand-new knowledge strategy dimension: (5) collaborative vs. competitive learning.

1.3.1. *Source of learning*

Internal learning occurs within the boundary of the firm. External learning depends on knowledge acquisition and transfer across firm boundaries. Extant literature suggests that internal learning is better for complex and systemic knowledge, due to more control over the development process and better understanding of the tacit nature of the knowledge (Chesbrough and Teece 1996). In contrast, external learning facilitates the development of a broader knowledge base and increases the flexibility of the firm, which is critical in a dynamic, competitive environment (Grant 1996b).

However, internal and external learning are also mutually interdependent and complementary (Cassiman and Veugelers 2006; Cohen and Levinthal 1990).

The most prominent characteristic of OSS sponsorship as a knowledge strategy may reside in its external learning orientation. Sponsoring firms are learning not only the explicit knowledge codified into software code, but also the innovative, large-scale collaborative software production processes exemplified by major OSS projects. This kind of learning can help the established firms to refresh their mindsets and catch up with the latest techniques in software engineering. Nevertheless, the effectiveness of this external learning orientation would at least in part depend on how well the firm can align externally gained knowledge with its internal learning processes to achieve the necessary balance (Durmusoglu *et al.* 2014).

1.3.2. *Degree of learning innovativeness*

The radicalness of learning refers to whether the learning processes focuses on incremental knowledge development built on current knowledge base, or path-breaking knowledge development in radically new areas. The former is good for short-term financial gains, while the latter can be critical for long-term survival. This dimension can be mapped readily into the exploitation vs. exploration dimension of knowledge strategy (Zack 1999).

OSS-based knowledge strategy may be either explorative or exploitative. While some firms leverage the open-source community as a learning channel to gain access to radically new knowledge, others may try to use this channel to influence the direction of the community (Dahlander and Wallin 2006). However, the latter case may exemplify more competitive than learning motives. Therefore, we may consider learning through OSS as largely radical rather than incremental. The effectiveness of such knowledge strategies depends on the perceived knowledge gap between firm's current knowledge base and its desired new knowledge base.

1.3.3. *Speed of learning*

The speed of learning is associated with the strategic choice between internal and external learning. Due to the lack of control over the learning process, as well as cognitive barriers such as "Not-invented-here" behavior (Katz and Allen 1982), external learning tends to be more costly and therefore slower than internal learning. Additionally, investment in fast learning may commit the firm too quickly into a particular technological trajectory, which may create undesirable lock-in effect in environments with high technological uncertainties (Bierly and Chakrabarti 1996).

OSS-based knowledge strategy facilitates fast learning, mainly due to the real-time feedback provided through the collaborative software development processes, including mailing-lists and online forums. The feedback from the open-source community may not only enhance the technology aspects of the product but more importantly allow the sponsoring firm to experiment at a relatively low cost and learn about the market potential of their future product offerings. In this sense, OSS-based knowledge strategy can be very effective in achieving first mover advantage, while at the same time avoiding the downside of technological lock-in (Zhu and Zhou 2011).

1.3.4. *Scope of knowledge base*

The breadth vs. depth tradeoff in a firm's knowledge base has major implications on its capabilities and performance. Extant literature has suggested that knowledge base depth, or a dedicated focus on a narrow-defined knowledge domain is a crucial factor for a firm to develop core competences (Prahalad and Hamel 1990). On the other hand, knowledge base breadth, or the degree of exposure to diverse knowledge domains, is positively associated with knowledge integration capabilities of the firm, which is the key to firm performance (Grant 1996a; Henderson and Cockburn 1994). Also, a broad knowledge base may result in strategic flexibility and adaptability necessary for survival in turbulent environments (Volberda 1996).

OSS-based knowledge strategy involves boundary-spanning efforts for external knowledge acquisition (O'Mahony and Bechky 2008). Given the dispersed nature of the open-source community, knowledge structures within them tend to be more diverse than narrow. Therefore, OSS-based knowledge strategies are most likely more effective in achieving knowledge base breadth rather than depth.

1.3.5. *Coopetition in learning*

As an extension to the knowledge strategy dimensions prescribed in the extant literature, the OSS production processes showcased a brand-new tension or potential tradeoff, between collaborative and competitive learning. The former is a learning mode involving knowledge sharing and common knowledge pool development, while the latter is more focused on knowledge protection and proprietary knowledge base building. In the collaborative learning mode, all participants make contributions to the common knowledge pool. Due to the non-rival nature of knowledge, all firms can benefit from a bigger knowledge pie. Conversely, in the competitive learning mode, firms are engaged in a learning race attempting to grow its own knowledge pie while protecting it from knowledge imitation by other competing firms, which may result in higher potential for profit appropriation, but lower level of knowledge base development.

OSS-based knowledge strategy is clearly favoring the collaborative learning over competitive learning. The open-source community is built on the premise of knowledge sharing (Barrett *et al.* 2013; Stewart and Gosain 2006), which has proven to be a successful model as far as knowledge base development is concerned. Firms may as well benefit from this collaborative learning model if they are willing to tradeoff certain profit appropriation for the benefit of knowledge acquisition.

1.3.6. *Summary*

In summary, the OSS-based knowledge strategy emphasizes external, radical, fast, and collaborative learning, in favor of a broad knowledge base. The ultimate goal of this OSS-based knowledge strategy is to achieve a balance between flexibility through external knowledge exploration with the help from the open-source community, and long-term performance improvement through development of new knowledge resources and capabilities. This view of OSS sponsorship as knowledge strategy not only sheds new light on this phenomenon itself, but more importantly, provides guidance for us to further investigate the underlying factors that may determine the heterogeneous performance outcomes of these open-source initiatives. In Table 2, we summarize on the

Table 2. OSS sponsorship as knowledge strategy.

Knowledge Strategy Dimensions	Description	OSS Knowledge Strategy
Source of learning	• Internal learning is good for complex, systemic, tacit knowledge. • External learning facilitates broader knowledge base and increases flexibility.	• Emphasizes external learning. • Its effect also depends on internal learning capabilities.
Degree of learning innovativeness	• Incremental learning builds on current knowledge base, which is good for short-term exploitation. • Radical learning involves pathbreaking knowledge exploration necessary for long-term survival.	• Some firms use OSS community for knowledge access. • Others use it to influence others in the community.
Speed of learning	• External learning is more costly and slower than internal learning. • Fast learning may prematurely commit a firm to a technological trajectory.	• Facilitates fast learning through quick feedback. • Also reduces the risk of lock-in due to experimentation enabled by OSS knowledge pool.
Scope of knowledge base	• Knowledge depth is the key to core competence development. • Knowledge breadth facilitates knowledge integration as well as flexibility.	• More effective in achieving knowledge breadth than depth
Coopetition in learning	• Collaborative learning focuses on knowledge sharing and common knowledge pool building. • Competitive learning focuses on protection of proprietary knowledge for profit appropriation.	• Emphasizes collaborative learning and knowledge sharing. • Aims at growing the OSS common knowledge pool.

relationships between knowledge strategy dimensions and the OSS knowledge strategy.

2. China's OSS Ecosystem

China's participation in the open-source ecosystem dates back to 1999, when the Chinese government supported the development of Linux systems in China (Ni 2006). However, only recently do we start to witness the substantial growth in China's open-source communities. For example, among the 40 million registered users of Github,[11] developers from China rank second in both numbers and OSS project contributions. Among all the active OSS contributors in China, more than 40% started to participate in the OSS ecosystem since 2019. Most of them are young developers born after 1990 and contribute to OSS ecosystem out of pure personal interests.[12]

Essentially, China's OSS ecosystem is still in its early stage of development, following the steps of the global open-source movement. Fortunately, the fast-growing Chinese ICT industry has paid attention to the open-source innovation model. Nowadays, many prominent Chinese ICT companies, including Huawei, Alibaba, Baidu and Tencent, etc., are actively contributing to the OSS ecosystem in China. Based on the 2018 world ranking of companies contributing most OSS projects to Github, the three Chinese Internet giants Baidu, Alibaba, and Tencent stood out. Alibaba ranks 9th with 694 employees, Tencent ranks 12th with 605 employees, and Baidu ranks 15th with 584 employees contributing to OSS projects on Github.[13]

OSS is of strategic importance to China, particularly amid the cutthroat economic and technology competition between the US and China today. For instance, the US government has imposed technology sanctions on China, including both hardware such as CPUs and software

---

[11]GitHub (github.com) is the world's largest repository of OSS projects, which allows developers from around the world to collaborate on OSS projects. The website URL is: https://github.com/.

[12]https://baijiahao.baidu.com/s?id=1653746261499289251&wfr=spider&for=pc.

[13]http://www.codertopic.com/?p=5613.

such as Google's Android operating system. As a result, Chinese companies such as Huawei are left with no choice but to resort to open-source hardware and software to overcome such difficulties. Therefore, with strong support from the Chinese government, OSS has regained huge momentum recently in China. Figure 1 illustrates the current status of China's OSS Ecosystem. As can be seen, the government-sponsored OSS usually uses the knowledge built in the global ecosystem, while the other two, grassroots developer and firm-sponsored OSS from China contribute back to the global ecosystem in addition to using the knowledge in it.

There have been many cases of successful open-source platforms in the making, from both large established companies, as well as the grassroot OSS communities in China. We will now examine some of the most prominent OSS innovations developed by Chinese companies today.

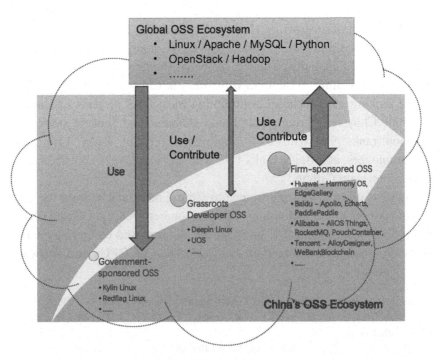

Figure 1. China's OSS ecosystem.

2.1. *Deepin Linux*

China's OSS ecosystem started around 1999, with Chinese government support for the adoption of the Linux operating system for national security concerns. As a result, many Chinese Linux distributions have been developed over the past two decades, including prominent ones such as Kylin Linux, Redflag Linux, iSoft Linux, etc. Most of these Linux distributions have been developed by government research institutions and state-owned enterprises. Typically, these Linux distributions are not sold to commercial customers, but rather used in academic institutions, government agencies, defense industries, etc. However, in recent years, major progress has been made in commercial Linux distributions in China, among which Deepin Linux is one of the most successful. According to DistroWatch,[14] Deepin Linux ranks among top 10 Linux distributions in the world, and number one in China. As of 2019, Deepin Linux supports 33 different languages, and has been downloaded over 80 million times by users across 6 continents.

Deepin Linux was initially started by grassroots OSS developers. The first distribution was released in 2008. The Deepin company was founded in 2011. In 2015, the company started commercial operations with over 100 employees, after securing venture financing of RMB 80 million in 2014.[15]

In terms of technology, Deepin Linux is developed based on Debian Linux. The product portfolio includes Deepin Desktop Environment, Deepin Server OS, Deepin Security OS, and over 30 Deepin self-developed application innovations. Deepin Linux leverages the dual-licensing business model, with the free community version and the for-profit commercial version. Also, Deepin provides various customized services for their commercial version. Typically, the customers of Deepin Linux are government agencies or banks. Furthermore, in recent years, Deepin has formed a strategic alliance with Huawei. Since September 2019, Huawei's laptops started to ship with pre-installed Deepin Desktop Environment,[16] which is highly customized for Chinese market, and suitable for daily office work as well as entertainment needs. Please see Figure 2 for the Deepin Desktop

---

[14]https://distrowatch.com/ is a website for news and feature lists of Linux and BSD distributions.
[15]USD to RMB exchange rate is around 6.8, as of November 2020.
[16]https://www.deepin.com/.

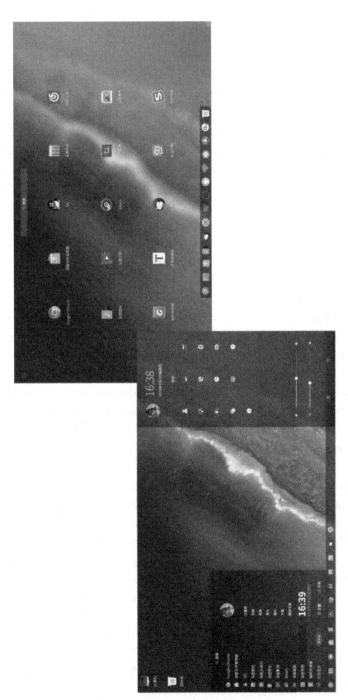

Figure 2.   Deepin desktop environment.

Environment, which is more elaborate than other desktop screens. Deepin's total revenue in 2018 was RMB 7.46 million.

As a keystone company in its OSS ecosystem, Deepin has been active in building its OSS community. As of November 2019, Deepin OSS community had over 90,000 registered members, including both companies and individual users. Total discussion posts exceed 605,400, with daily discussions around 500. Total feedback exceeds 4,327. The Deepin OSS community has great diversity, with 105 websites distributed over 33 countries in 6 continents. Deepin OSS ecosystem has its own application store, with thousands of applications including self-developed ones. Its application store is easy to use with one-click installation. The applications include high quality, comprehensive work and entertainment applications. Deepin Linux also supports many Windows applications through its Deepin-Wine technology. The strategic alliance with Huawei is another strength of Deepin. For example, Deepin participated in the development for Huawei's Kunpeng CPU, based on ARM architecture. Several Deepin server operating systems have been released in support of Huawei Taishan servers. Deepin also collaborated with many data base and office software vendors in China, in order to build up its OSS ecosystem.

Given the urgent need for China's future operating system market, Deepin is collaborating with other major OSS companies in China, in a joint effort to develop a new operating system called UOS. Hopefully this will allow China's OSS developers to have a common platform to develop on, to avoid fragmentation, to customize for China's own CPU hardware, and to improve coordination in building a more comprehensive and complete OSS ecosystem in China.[17]

2.2. *Huawei's harmony OS*

2.2.1. *Internet-of-Things*

According to International Telecommunication Union, the "Internet of Things" (IoT) connects everything on the Internet, using radio frequency automatic identification (RFID), wireless data communication, and other

---

[17]https://xueqiu.com/9231373161/156547231.

technologies. In this IoT network, goods (commodities) can "communicate" with each other without human intervention. Its essence is to use RFID technology to realize the automatic identification of articles (commodities), the interconnection and sharing of information through the Internet.

The value of IoT lies in the following: (1) Improve efficiency: Sensors can now be directly connected and integrated into enterprise systems. The valuable data in real time can be used to estimate, analyze, and inform decision-making processes to improve the production process, adjust its development and production cycles and responsiveness according to the demands. (2) Avoid loss and accident: More robust safety measures in autonomous vehicles and smart transport infrastructure could reduce the RMB 298 billion annual cost for traffic incidents. (3) Promote consumption: IoT applied in smart devices, TV set, and vehicles will bring out new and upgraded products, including wearables, connected car, and smart TV. (4) Create new business opportunities: The real value of IoT lies in the production, capture, and analysis of real time data, and the possibility of using this data for social good. This is promoting business innovation, such as IoT data analysis. Many new start-up companies are emerging, creating new business models, and employment opportunities for the society.

The architecture of IoT can be divided into four layers: device layer, network layer, platform layer, and application layer, as illustrated in Figure 3.

2.2.2. Harmony OS

In August 2019, Huawei officially announced its Harmony OS, which is intended to be its cross-platform operating system for IoT. It is a cutting-edge open-source operating system based on microkernel technology. In the next few years, Harmony OS will be adopted in a wide range of devices including smartphones, tablet PCs, smart TVs, smart cars, and wearable devices. More importantly, Harmony OS serves as Huawei's backup plan for Android, which would no longer be available for Huawei's smartphones, amid technology sanctions from the US government. Therefore, Harmony OS may become a potential substitute for the

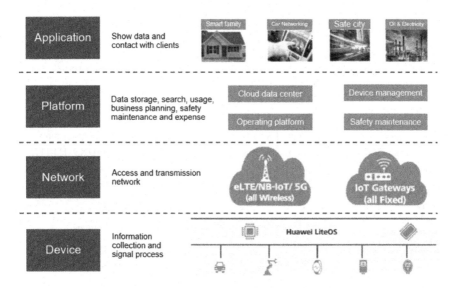

Figure 3.   Illustration of a typical IoT architecture.

Android operating system[18] on smartphones. In fact, its real target competitor is Google's next generation IoT operating system, Fuchsia OS.[19] Table 3 compares the main features of Harmony OS (as of version 1.2) vs. Fuchsia OS. As we can see from Table 3, Harmony OS and Fuchsia OS are both next generation, microkernel-based IoT operating systems, which are more future-oriented than Android. They are similar in terms of both technological architecture features and target markets. The main difference is that Harmony OS currently has more proprietary components and focus more on security. Yet with the further open sourcing of Harmony OS, we may expect to see more open components being incorporated in it in the future.

The development of Harmony OS dates back to 2012, when Huawei started the research and development on its lightweight IoT operating system LiteOS, which is also an open-source system. In the future, LiteOS will be gradually merged into Harmony OS to become part of its device access layer. In 2017, Harmony OS completed its initial technology

---

[18] https://hmxt.org/.
[19] https://fuchsia-china.com/.

Table 3.   Comparison between Harmony OS and Google Fuchsia OS.[a]

Feature	Harmony OS	Fuchsia OS
Kernel	Currently (version 1.0) Linux Kernel + LiteOS + Microkernel. In the future pure Microkernel only	Zircon Microkernel
Inter-process communication (IPC)	Distributed Soft Bus, with proprietary mini protocol and SDK	Open protocols: such as IPv6, mDNS, HTTP/2.0
Code compatibility	POSIX	POSIX
CPU	ARM	ARM, x86
Devices	All IoT devices	All IoT devices
Security	Trusted Execution Environment (TEE)	Capability-based security mechanism
VR/AR engine	N/A	Escher
Real time support	Priority-based scheduling	Hard real time engine

Note: [a]https://www.zhihu.com/question/340032996/answer/784807496.

feasibility test. After that, in 2019, Harmony OS 1.0 was announced, along with the first product incorporating it — Honor Smart TV, which can serve as the control center of smart homes in the future. According to Huawei's plan, in the next two years, Harmony OS will be upgraded with microkernel and application frameworks, etc. It will be incorporated into various devices including personal computers, smart watches, headphones, virtual reality glasses, and more. The architecture of Harmony OS is illustrated in Figure 4.

Harmony OS has the following key technological advantages:

(1) *Distributed architecture*: Leveraging features such as a public communication platform, distributed data management, distributed capability scheduling, and virtual external devices, developers may focus on their own business logic without dealing with the challenges of implementing distributed computing themselves. As a result, they can develop cross-platform applications in the same way as developing single-device applications, while being able to deploy to various

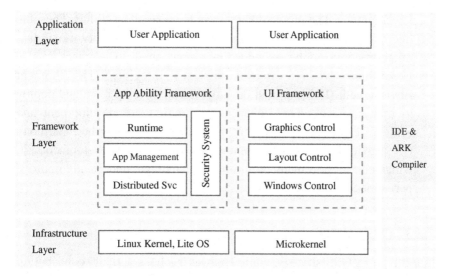

Figure 4. Harmony OS architecture.

platforms. At the same time, users may enjoy seamless user experiences across devices. In addition, such distributed architecture facilitates stability and reliability. If one component of the system becomes dysfunctional, the whole system can still function by quickly switching to backup components.

(2) *Smooth performance*: Harmony OS has a finite latency engine, which can analyze and predict working load in real time, to achieve optimal resource allocation, reduce latency, and ensure high performance. Also, Harmony OS improved its inter-process communication (IPC) performance. Compared with Google's Fuchsia, Harmony OS IPC performance is about five times faster.

(3) *Microkernel*: Harmony OS leverages sophisticated microkernel technology to enhance system security. Microkernel design can simplify the functionalities of the system kernel, so that the kernel only provides most foundational services such as IPC and process scheduling, while other services are provided by external modules. Harmony OS applies microkernel technology to create a Trustworthy Execution Environment (TEE) and reduces its code size to 1/1000 of Linux kernel. As a result, Harmony OS can achieve much higher security and

lower latency. The minimal kernel can be as small as 10 KB. Thus, the microkernel design facilitates compatibility, extensibility, flexibility, reliability, and can be embedded into many small IoT devices.

(4) *Ecosystem sharing*: Huawei provides Integrated Development Environment (IDE), so that developers can develop once and deploy to many devices. This enhances productivity of development and achieves cross-platform sharing in the ecosystem. Further, Harmony OS provides the ARK compiler and distributed development kit, which can support many programming languages and greatly improve performance.

2.2.3. OSS platform ecosystem strategy

In terms of its OSS strategy, while Huawei has been actively contributing to OSS communities, such as Linux system patching (ranking #1 in China, and #7 among global companies), Harmony OS is perhaps the biggest OSS platform endeavor that Huawei ever attempted. The motivation is two-fold. First, in the long term, IoT is where the future opportunities reside. Huawei is aiming to capture the IoT market with its Harmony OS. Second, in the short term, there is the urgent need to replace Google Android platform, which will soon become unavailable to Huawei due to the US sanctions. Huawei has no choice, but to develop its own smartphone operating system. This is a huge challenge to Huawei, because it was accustomed to be a hardware company. Yet now the only way for Huawei to survive is to build a software ecosystem. To have even a slim chance competing with market leaders like the open-source Android platform, open source is the only way to go for Harmony OS, given its ability to gain wide adoption and to build a platform ecosystem as discussed previously. So far, Huawei has already open sourced its ARK compiler and the LiteOS. Eventually, Huawei promises to open source the entire Harmony OS platform.[20] In that regard, Huawei's OSS knowledge strategy resembles one where it is using OSS community for knowledge access.

Huawei's IoT ecosystem follows the "1+8+N" strategy, which consists of three parts: one core entrance (mobile phone), eight auxiliary

---

[20]https://hmxt.org/%E9%B8%BF%E8%92%99%E7%B3%BB%E7%BB%9Ffaq.

entrances (e.g., speakers, headphones, watches, tablets, etc.), and N refers to everything that can be connected to the Internet. In order to maintain ecosystem health, Huawei will only focus on the "1+8" part, leaving the "N" opportunities to other companies. Rather, Huawei will focus on the construction and promotion of its IoT infrastructures in the platform layer. From the development of the underlying operating system platform to the manufacturing of IoT chips, Huawei has made tremendous contribution to its IoT ecosystem, which empowers numerous small business partners to develop their own applications and co-create value within this IoT platform ecosystem built by Huawei.

So far, Harmony OS has gained wide-spread support from both domestic and foreign companies. Huawei has signed strategic alliance agreements with influential domestic partners including Chinasoft International (Software solutions),[21] iFlytek (Voice recognition software),[22] 360 (Internet security),[23] Digital China (IT service),[24] etc. Foreign partners include social network giants like Facebook, Instagram, and Twitter.[25] As of August 2020, the Harmony OS platform ecosystem has accumulated over 550,000 applications, and over 1.3 million developers worldwide. Overall, this is a remarkable achievement for Huawei.

3. Conclusion and Future Outlook

OSS represents a new open innovation paradigm that has become prevalent in the technology industries worldwide. After 20 years of development, OSS 2.0 has matured into a mainstream business model for most technology companies, even for Microsoft. At the same time, global OSS community also reached a plateau, as evidenced by slower growth in terms of new OSS projects in recent years, due to the mature stage of the OSS movement.

---

[21] http://www.chinasofti.com/.
[22] https://www.iflytek.com/en/.
[23] http://www.360totalsecurity.com/.
[24] http://www.digitalchina.com/en/.
[25] https://dy.163.com/article/FL222PFF05313F8T.html?referFrom=baidu.

Although China is a late comer to the scene, it has quickly become one of the fastest growing OSS markets in recent years. There are reasons beyond technology, such as concerns for national security, especially in the current context of US–China tensions from trade to technology. On the other hand, from the perspective of knowledge strategy, OSS can be leveraged by commercial firms to facilitate innovation as well as market competition. It is particularly useful in gaining widespread adoption and building platform ecosystems. In this sense, Chinese companies like Huawei are actively leveraging OSS to build their platform ecosystems. Such contribution by Chinese companies to the global OSS community would be a win–win for both parties.

Based on our case study of OSS innovation in China, we may see the following unique characteristics, among others: (1) Although fast-growing, China's OSS ecosystem is still in an early phase of development. The OSS community culture norms, such as collaboration, reciprocity, charity, and respect for property rights are still lacking. (2) OSS is gaining importance in China, partly due to US–China tensions in trade and technology. National security concerns serve as a major driver of government support for OSS, which is crucial for OSS growth in China. (3) There has been a paradigm shift in terms of how Chinese companies leverage OSS. In the past, OSS, such as Linux, was mainly considered as standalone innovation. Nowadays, with the intensification of platform ecosystem-based competition, the unique advantages of OSS platforms in building platform ecosystems are being recognized, which is clearly illustrated in the case of Huawei's Harmony OS.

The OSS ecosystem in China is flourishing today and will continue to grow in the future. With OSS, Chinese firms can build their open platform ecosystems to attract large number of third-party complementors to co-create complex technology products that are competitive in the global market. At the same time, these companies are contributing back to the global OSS ecosystem, in the spirit of reciprocity as well as to sustain its healthy growth. This is exactly what Huawei is trying to achieve with its Harmony OS, and many other OSS initiatives such as its participation in the Linux Foundation. Further, more and more Chinese firms are joining the global OSS ecosystems and making their contribution, including not only the technology giants such as Baidu, Alibaba, Tencent, ByteDance, and

Huawei but also many Chinese startup firms which build their products on top of various OSS platforms in AI, big data, cloud technologies, etc.

While substantial progress has been made in China's OSS ecosystem, there are also many risks and challenges. First and foremost, compared with developed countries like the US, the OSS-based business model has not been widely adopted by Chinese companies. Except for a few Linux vendors with support from the Chinese government, there are still too few companies in China dedicated to OSS development. More collaboration and cultivation are urgently needed in China's OSS market. Secondly, the Chinese OSS communities are underdeveloped. Most Chinese OSS projects are sponsored by companies, developed within their internal environment, based on a closed innovation model. This essentially goes against the open innovation principle of OSS development. Further, OSS ecosystem has its own rules regarding property rights (e.g., GPL). As mentioned previously, there rules are not well respected and protected in China. Opportunistic OSS developers in China sometimes conceal their software codes after development leveraging OSS codes, which not only undermines the culture of code sharing and giving back in global OSS communities, but also violates the GPL rules. These issues need to be addressed before China's OSS ecosystem can see healthy growth in the future.

Overall, Chinese companies may benefit from the open innovation in the OSS ecosystem, while the OSS community worldwide can benefit from fresh innovation contributions made by developers from the most populous country in the world. Even though OSS communities in China are still underdeveloped and face many challenges due to its immaturity, the future looks promising.

References

Adner, R. (2017). Ecosystem as structure an actionable construct for strategy, *Journal of Management*, 43(1), 39–58.

Adner, R. and Kapoor, R. (2015). Innovation ecosystems and the pace of substitution: Re-examining technology S-curves, *Strategic Management Journal*, 37(4), 625–648.

Alexy, O., West, J., Klapper, H., and Reitzig, M. (2018). Surrendering control to gain advantage: Reconciling openness and the resource-based view of the firm, *Strategic Management Journal*, 39(6), 1704–1727.

Almirall, E. and Casadesus-Masanell, R. (2010). Open versus closed innovation: A model of discovery and divergence, *Academy of Management Review*, 35(1), 27–47.

Arthur, W. (1989). Competing technologies, increasing returns, and lock-in by historical events, *The Economic Journal*, 99(394), 116–131.

Baldwin, C. and von Hippel, E. (2011). Modeling a paradigm shift: From producer innovation to user and open collaborative innovation, *Organization Science*, 22(6), 1399–1417.

Barrett, M., Heracleous, L., and Walsham, G. (2013). A rhetorical approach to IT diffusion: Reconceptualizing the ideology-framing relationship in computerization movements, *Mis Quarterly*, 201–220.

Behlendorf, B. (1999). Open source as a business strategy, *Open Sources: Voices from the Open Source Revolution*. Online book from O'Reilly Media.

Bergquist, M. and Ljungberg, J. (2001). The power of gifts: Organizing social relationships in open source communities, *Information Systems Journal*, 11(4), 305–320.

Bierly, P. and Chakrabarti, A. (1996). Generic knowledge strategies in the U.S. pharmaceutical industry, *Strategic Management Journal*, 17(Winter), 123–135.

Bogers, M., Zobel, A.-K., Afuah, A., Almirall, E., Brunswicker, S., Dahlander, L., Frederiksen, L., Gawer, A., Gruber, M., and Haefliger, S. (2017). The open innovation research landscape: Established perspectives and emerging themes across different levels of analysis, *Industry and Innovation*, 24(1), 8–40.

Bonaccorsi, A., Giannangeli, S., and Rossi, C. (2006). Entry strategies under competing standards: Hybrid business models in the OSS industry, *Management Science*, 52(7), 1085–1098.

Bonaccorsi, A. and Rossi, C. (2006). Comparing motivations of individual programmers and firms to take part in the open source movement: From community to business, *Knowledge, Technology and Policy*, 18(4), 40–64.

Boudreau, K. (2010). Open platform strategies and innovation: Granting access versus devolving control, *Management Science*, 56(10), 1849–1872.

Cassiman, B. and Veugelers, R. (2006). In search of complementarity in innovation strategy: Internal R&D and external knowledge acquisition, *Management Science*, 52(1), 68–82.

Chesbrough, H. and Teece, D. (1996). When is virtual virtuous? Organizing for Innovation, *Harvard Business Review*, 74(1), 65–74.

Cohen, W. M. and Levinthal, D. A. (1990). Absorptive capacity: A new perspective on learning and innovation, *Administrative Science Quarterly*, 35(1), 128–152.

Colombo, M. G., Piva, E., and Rossi-Lamastra, C. (2014). Open innovation and within-industry diversification in small and medium enterprises: The case of OSS firms, *Research Policy*, 43(5), 891–902.

Curto-Millet, D. and Shaikh, M. (2017). The emergence of openness in open-source projects: The case of open her, *Journal of Information Technology*, 32(4), 361–379.

Dahlander, L. (2007). Penguin in a new suit: A tale of how de novo entrants emerged to harness free and OSS communities, *Industrial and Corporate Change*, 16(5), 913–943.

Dahlander, L. and Magnusson, M. (2008). How do firms make use of open source communities? *Long Range Planning*, 41(6), 629–649.

Dahlander, L. and Wallin, M. W. (2006). A man on the inside: Unlocking communities as complementary assets, *Research Policy*, 35(8), 1243–1259.

Dahlander, L., Frederiksen, L., and Rullani, F. (2008). Online communities and open innovation: Governance and symbolic value creation, *Industry and Innovation*, 15(2), 115–123.

Dalle, J.-M. and Jullien, N. (2003). "Libre" software: Turning fads into institutions? *Research Policy*, 32(1), 1–11.

Daniel, S. L., Maruping, L. M., Cataldo, M., and Herbsleb, J. (2018). The impact of ideology misfit on OSS communities and companies, *MIS Quarterly*, 42(4), 1069–1096.

David, P. A. and Rullani, F. (2008). Dynamics of innovation in an "open source" collaboration environment: Lurking, laboring, and launching FLOSS projects on SourceForge, *Industrial and Corporate Change*, 17(4), 647–710.

Di Tullio, D. and Staples, D. S. (2013). The governance and control of OSS projects, *Journal of Management Information Systems*, 30(3), 49–80.

DiDio, L. (2005). 2005 North American Linux and Windows TCO Comparison, Part 1. The Yankee Group Report, April 2005, Boston, MA.

Durmusoglu, S., Jacobs, M., Nayir, D., Khilji, S., and Wang, X. (2014). The quasi-moderating role of organizational culture in the relationship between rewards and knowledge transfer: Evidence from a European multinational firm, *Journal of Knowledge Management*, 18(1), 19–37.

Fitzgerald, B. (2006). The transformation of OSS, *MIS Quarterly*, 30(3), 587–598.

Fosfuri, A., Giarratana, M. S., and Luzzi, A. (2008). The penguin has entered the building: The commercialization of OSS products, *Organization Science*, 19(2), 292–305.

Franke, N. and von Hippel, E. (2003). Satisfying heterogeneous user needs via innovation toolkits: The case of Apache security software, *Research Policy*, 32(7), 1199–1215.

Gawer, A. (2014). Bridging differing perspectives on technological platforms: Toward an integrative framework, *Research Policy*, 43(7), 1239–1249.

Goldman, R. and Gabriel, R. (2005). *Innovation Happens Elsewhere: Open Source as Business Strategy*, San Francisco: Morgan Kaufmann Publishers.

Grand, S., von Krogh, G., Leonard, D., and Swap, W. (2004). Resource allocation beyond firm boundaries: A multi-level model for open source innovation, *Long Range Planning*, 37(6), 591–610.

Grant, R. (1996a). Toward a knowledge-based theory of the firm, *Strategic Management Journal*, 17(10), 109–122.

Grant, R. (1996b). Prospering in dynamically-competitive environments: Organizational capability as knowledge integration, *Organization Science*, 7(4), 375–387.

Grewal, R., Lilien, G. L., and Mallapragada, G. (2006). Location, location, location: How network embeddedness affects project success in open source systems, *Management Science*, 52(7), 1043–1056.

Hahn, J., Moon, J., and Zhang, C. (2008). Emergence of new project teams from OSS developer networks: Impact of prior collaboration ties, *Information Systems Research*, 19(3), 369–391.

Harison, E. and Koski, H. (2010). Applying open innovation in business strategies: Evidence from Finnish software firms, *Research Policy*, 39(3), 351–359.

Hauge, Ø., Sørensen, C.-F., and Conradi, R. (2008). Adoption of open source in the software industry, *Open Source Development, Communities and Quality*, 275, 211–221.

Henderson, R. and Cockburn, I. (1994). Measuring competence? Exploring firm effects in pharmaceutical research, *Strategic Management Journal*, 15(S1), 63–84.

Henkel, J. (2006). Selective revealing in open innovation processes: The case of embedded Linux, *Research Policy*, 35(7), 953–969.

Henkel, J. (2009). Champions of revealing — The role of open source developers in commercial firms, *Ind Corp Change*, 18(3), 435–471.

Katz, R. and Allen, T. (1982). Investigating the Not Invented Here (NIH) syndrome: A look at the performance, tenure, and communication patterns of 50 R & D Project Groups, *R&D Management*, 12(1), 7–20.

Katz, M. and Shapiro, C. (1985). Network externalities, competition, and compatibility, *The American Economic Review*, 75(3), 424–440.

Kogut, B. and Zander, U. (1992). Knowledge of the firm, combinative capabilities, and the replication of technology, *Organization Science*, 3(3), 383–397.

Krishnamurthy, S., Ou, S. S., and Tripathi, A. K. (2014). Acceptance of monetary rewards in OSS development, *Research Policy*, 43(4), 632–644.

Kuk, G. (2006). Strategic interaction and knowledge sharing in the KDE developer mailing List, *Management Science*, 52(7), 1031–1042.

Lakhani, K. and Wolf, R. (2005). Why hackers do what they do: Understanding motivation and effort in free/OSS projects. In *Perspectives in Free and OSS*, eds. J. Feller, B. Fitzgerald, S. Hissam, and K. Lakhani, pp. 3–21. Cambridge, MA: MIT Press.

Lakhani, K. R. and von Hippel, E. (2003). How OSS works: "Free" user-to-user assistance, *Research Policy*, 32(6), 923–943.

Lerner, J., Pathak, P. A., and Tirole, J. (2006). The dynamics of open-source contributors, *The American Economic Review*, 96(2), 114–118.

Lerner, J. and Schankerman, M. (2010). *The Comingled Code: Open Source and Economic Development*, Cambridge, MA: MIT Press.

Lerner, J. and Tirole, J. (2001). The open source movement: Key research questions, *European Economic Review*, 45(4–6), 819–826.

Lerner, J. and Tirole, J. (2002). Some simple economics of open source, *Journal of Industrial Economics*, 50(2), 197–218.

Lerner, J. and Tirole, J. (2005). The scope of open source licensing, *Journal of Law Economics and Organization*, 21(1), 20–56.

Liebeskind, J. P. (1996). Knowledge, strategy, and the theory of the firm, *Strategic Management Journal*, 17(Winter), 93–107.

Lindberg, A., Berente, N., Gaskin, J., and Lyytinen, K. (2016). Coordinating interdependencies in online communities: A study of an OSS project, *Information Systems Research*, 27(4), 751–772.

MacCormack, A., Rusnak, J., and Baldwin, C. Y. (2006). Exploring the structure of complex software designs: An empirical study of open source and proprietary code, *Management Science*, 52(7), 1015–1030.

Ndofor, H. and Levitas, E. (2004). Signaling the strategic value of knowledge, *Journal of Management*, 30(5), 685–702.

Ni, G. (2006). Open source: The way out for Chinese software, *Software World*, 14, 20–21.

O'Mahony, S. and Bechky, B. A. (2008). Boundary organizations: Enabling collaboration among unexpected allies, *Administrative Science Quarterly*, 53(3), 422–459.

O'Mahony, S. and Ferraro, F. (2007). The emergence of governance in an open source community, *Academy of Management Journal*, 50(5), 1079–1106.

O'Mahony, S. and Karp, R. (2020). From proprietary to collective governance: How do platform participation strategies evolve? *Strategic Management Journal*, Special Issue Article, 1–33. https://doi.org/10.1002/smj.3150.

Osterloh, M. and Rota, S. (2007). OSS development — Just another case of collective invention? *Research Policy*, 36(2), 157–171.

Pisano, G. (2006). Profiting from innovation and the intellectual property revolution, *Research Policy*, 35(8), 1122–1130.

Pitt, L. F., Watson, R. T., Berthon, P., Wynn, D., and Zinkhan, G. (2006). The Penguin's window: Corporate brands from an open-source perspective, *Journal of the Academy of Marketing Science*, 34(2), 115–127.

Prahalad, C. K. and Hamel, G. (1990). The core competence of the corporation, *Harvard Business Review*, 68(3), 79–91.

Raymond, E. (1999). *The Cathedral and the Bazaar: Musings on Linux and Open Source by an Accidental Revolutionary*, Cambridge, MA: O'Reilly.

Roberts, J. A., Il-Horn, H., and Slaughter, S. A. (2006). Understanding the motivations, participation, and performance of OSS developers: A longitudinal study of the Apache projects, *Management Science*, 52(7), 984–999.

Schilling, M. (1999). Winning the standards race: Building installed base and the availability of complementary goods, *European Management Journal*, 17(3), 265–274.

Setia, P., Bayus, B. L., and Rajagopalan, B. (2020). The takeoff of OSS: A signaling perspective based on community activities, *MIS Quarterly*, 44(3).

Shah, S. K. (2006). Motivation, governance, and the viability of hybrid forms in OSS development, *Management Science*, 52(7), 1000–1014.

Simon, K. D. (2005). The value of open standards and open-source software in government environments, *IBM Systems Journal*, 44(2), 227–238.

Stam, W. (2009). When does community participation enhance the performance of OSS companies? *Research Policy*, 38(8), 1288–1299.

Stam, W. and Elfring, T. (2008). Entrepreneurial orientation and new venture performance: The moderating role of intra- and extraindustry social capital, *Academy of Management Journal*, 51(1), 97–111.

Stewart, K. J. and Gosain, S. (2006). The impact of ideology on effectiveness in OSS development teams, *MIS Quarterly*, 30(2), 291–314.

Stuermer, M., Spaeth, S., and von Krogh, G. (2009). Extending private-collective innovation: A case study, *R&D Management*, 39(2), 170–191.

Teece, D. J. (1986). Profiting from technological innovation: Implications for integration, collaboration, licensing and public policy, *Research Policy*, 15(6), 285–305.

Teece, D. J. (2006). Reflections on "profiting from innovation", *Research Policy*, 35(8), 1131–1146.

Volberda, H. W. (1996). Toward the flexible form: How to remain vital in hypercompetitive environments, *Organization Science*, 7(4), 359–374.

von Hippel, E. (2001). Innovation by user communities: Learning from open-source software (cover story), *MIT Sloan Management Review*, 42(4), 82–86.

von Hippel, E. and von Krogh, G. (2003). OSS and the "private-collective" innovation model: Issues for organization science, *Organization Science*, 14(2), 209–223.

Wen, W., Ceccagnoli, M., and Forman, C. (2016). Opening up intellectual property strategy: Implications for OSS entry by start-up firms, *Management Science*, 62(9), 2668–2691.

West, J. (2003). How open is open enough? Melding proprietary and open source platform strategies, *Research Policy*, 32(7), 1259–1285.

West, J. and Gallagher, S. (2006). Challenges of open innovation: The paradox of firm investment in open-source software, *R&D Management*, 36(3), 319–331.

Zack, M. H. (1999). Developing a knowledge strategy, *California Management Review*, 41(3), 125–145.

Zeitlyn, D. (2003). Gift economies in the development of OSS: Anthropological reflections, *Research Policy*, 32(7), 1287–1291.

Zhu, K. X. and Zhou, Z. Z. (2011). Lock-in strategy in software competition: Open-source software vs. proprietary software, *Information Systems Research*, 23(2), 536–545.

Localization in Business-to-Consumer Cross-Border Online Marketplaces: How AliExpress Turkey Enables Its Sellers' Brands and Manages Their Experiences

Yaman Alpata and Serdar S. Durmusoglu

1. Introduction

Firms both from emerging markets and developed markets face capability deficiencies as they vie for market leadership in the global marketplace. However, firms from emerging markets, especially small- and medium-sized enterprises (SMEs), lack different capabilities than those from developed markets. For example, SMEs founded in emerging markets significantly lack international marketing experience and own or sell brands with low brand equities (Ramamurti and Williamson 2019).

E-commerce, which refers to transactions of goods and services through electronic communications (Tian and Stewart 2006), may facilitate SMEs' reach to customers beyond their home country borders. However, selling across borders is a daunting task, especially because the SMEs have to overcome the challenges of not possessing established firm and/or brand names. SMEs face other resource and capability constraints and therefore many prefer using e-commerce platforms, also known as online marketplaces, when selling their products internationally. As a result, a deeper understanding of how these business-to-consumer (B2C) cross-border marketplaces localize their services, enhance the sellers' brands and manage their user experiences are phenomena that many aspiring SMEs as well as other online marketplaces should grasp to sustain competitive advantage. In particular, research finds that website localization and cultural customization improves website navigation, attitudes toward the site, and ultimately, higher purchase intentions (Singh 2011).

Localization of cross-border services is multifaceted and also include "web localization", which refers to "the adaptation of digital content on the web and through mobile applications or software applications to meet the cultural, linguistic, legal, and other requirements of a target market where it will be deployed" (Benmamoun *et al.* 2021, p. 216). Hence, many obstacles, such as brand language localization problem, may arise during localization (de la Cova 2021). In this chapter, we provide some lessons learned by AliExpress in Turkey, a subsidiary of Alibaba Group, when localizing their services.

The remainder of this chapter is organized as follows: first, we give an overview of Alibaba Group, describing some of its milestones. Then, we summarize the evolution of AliExpress, with specific attention to AliExpress' operations in Turkey, an emerging market. Next, we describe the five essential steps of successful design localization. We end the chapter with some concluding remarks on how other emerging B2C cross-border e-commerce platforms can benefit from the guidelines delineated in this chapter.

2. Alibaba Group: An Overview

Alibaba Group was established in 1999 as an online business-to-business (B2B) marketplace where buyers and sellers from around the world can connect and carry out transactions. For example, a firm in Chile can find a manufacturer in China and have goods produced and shipped to it. From the outset, the company's founders shared a belief that the Internet would level the playing field by enabling SMEs to leverage innovation and technology to grow and compete more effectively both in domestic and global markets. Since launching its first website, helping SMEs in China to sell internationally, Alibaba Group has grown into a vast digital ecosystem with businesses comprising core commerce, cloud computing, digital media and entertainment, and innovation initiatives. Figure 1 presents milestones in Alibaba Group's journey since its inception.

All participants in Alibaba Group's digital ecosystem — consumers, merchants, third-party service providers, and others — have an opportunity to prosper. Alibaba Group's success and rapid growth is built on the spirit of entrepreneurship, innovation, and an unwavering focus on meeting the needs of its customers whether businesses or end consumers. As can be seen in Figure 2 and Table 1, today, Alibaba Group's e-commerce business units (e.g., Taobao, Tmall, Tmall Global, AliExpress, and Lazada) serve both global as well as focused geographical markets.[1] By 2019, around 2.5 billion products were listed by 8.7 million sellers and manufacturers on Alibaba's China Retail Marketplaces, which make up 90% of smartphones and 90% of computers, 80% of wigs, 75% of toys in a global scale.

3. AliExpress

AliExpress, launched in 2010, is a global B2C cross-border retail marketplace that enables consumers outside of China, but from more than 200 countries and territories, to buy directly from manufacturers and distributors. AliExpress is powered by the Alibaba Group's ecosystem, consolidating expertise and experience from logistics to payments, digital marketing technologies to advanced translation algorithms (instant translation to 18 languages), globally designed campaigns such as 11.11 Global Shopping Festival to 7/24 online customer hotline services. AliExpress' mission is "making business easy to do anywhere".

---

[1]For a more detailed overview of Alibaba's businesses, please refer to Zeng (2018).

1999 – Alibaba is founded in Jack Ma's apartment in Hangzhou, Zhejiang, China, started operating a B2B marketplace, Alibaba.com, which connects Chinese and foreign suppliers to foreign wholesale buyers.
  – Another B2B marketplace, currently known as 1688.com, is launched for domestic (i.e., China) wholesale trade.
2000 – SoftBank Group Corp., which primarily funds technology, energy, and financial industries, invests $20 million in Alibaba.
2001 – Alibaba creates the mission, vision, and values that still drive the company today.
  – Alibaba.com surpasses 1 million registered users.
2002 – Online shopping platform Taobao Marketplace is founded, again, in Jack Ma's apartment.
2004 – Alipay's digital payment and escrow services are launched.
2009 – Alibaba Group enters cloud computing (Alibabacloud).
  – Alibaba Group holds the first 11.11 Global Shopping Festival.
2010 – One of Alibaba's global consumer marketplaces, AliExpress, is launched.
2011 – Alibaba Group establishes the Alibaba Foundation, which is dedicated to social causes.
2013 – Together with its logistics business partners, Alibaba Group establishes Cainiao Network and aims to fulfill consumer orders within 24 hours in China and within 72 hours elsewhere in the world.
2014 – Tmall Global is launched to enable international brands to offer products directly to consumers in China.
  – Alibaba Group goes public on the New York Stock Exchange.
2016 – Alibaba revolutionizes online and offline shopping with "New Retail", a term Alibaba coined to describe the meshing of online and offline commerce by digitizing the entire retail value chain to provide benefits for both the merchant and the consumer. Grocery shopping gets a New Retail makeover with the launch of Freshippo, a self-operated retail chain.
  – Alibaba acquires a controlling stake in Lazada.
2017 – Alibaba acquires a controlling stake in Cainiao Network and increases its stake in Lazada.
2018 – Alibaba participates in its first Olympic Games as a Top Partner in PyeongChang, South Korea.
  – Ele.me and Koubei are integrated into Alibaba Group's local consumer services business.
2019 – Alibaba Group turns 20.
  – Alibaba Group is officially listed on the Main Board of the Hong Kong Stock Exchange.
2020 – Alibaba ecosystem's total gross merchandise volume (GMV) surpasses US$1 trillion for fiscal year 2020.

Figure 1.   Alibaba Group's milestones.

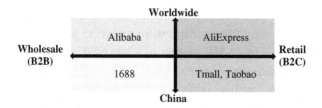

Figure 2. Alibaba group e-commerce business units (Geographical markets vs. types of markets served).

Table 1. Alibaba group e-commerce business units.

Business Unit	Website	Type	Geographical Markets Served	Year Started
Alibaba	Alibaba.com	B2B	Global, including China	1999
1688	1688.com	B2B	China	1999
Taobao	Taobao.com	B2C	China	2003
Tmall	Tmall.com	B2C	China	2008
Tmall global*	Shopglobal.com	B2C	China	2014
AliExpress	Aliexpress.com	B2C	Global, except China	2010
Lazada	Lazada.com	B2C	Southeast Asia	2012
Daraz	Daraz.com	B2C	South Asia (Pakistan, Bangladesh, Sri Lanka, Myanmar, and Nepal)	2012

Note: *Merchants in Tmall (sometimes referred to as "Tmall Classic") are entities in China with products registered in China. On the other hand, Tmall Global sellers are firms with corporate entities outside of China and sell imported products in China.

This is highly consistent with Alibaba Group's vision of building the future infrastructure of commerce. AliExpress' key value propositions are value for money, where it shortens supply chain by directly connecting manufacturers with global consumers and broad product selection,[2] which exceeds 100 million. Currently, AliExpress' global

---

[2]Product selection = Stock product unit, i.e., SPU (e.g., A T-shirt is considered as one SPU; if a particular T-shirt has three sizes and three different color offerings, then it has nine stock keeping units (SKU)).

Alexa ranking[3] is 45 as of June 30, 2021 and by the end of 2019, more than 60% of buyers on the platform were under 35 years old.

Acknowledging that SME success is achieved if global infrastructure is coupled with localized services and know how, AliExpress opened its platform to vendors in countries other than in China. Previously, only Chinese sellers were allowed on the platform and were able to sell their products anywhere but China. In 2019, SMEs in Russia, Turkey, Italy, and Spain were able to register and sell their products via AliExpress network. Among these, Turkey had a special positioning as the SMEs could sell and ship globally like Chinese sellers, where other overseas sellers could sell only locally or regionally. For example, Russian sellers could only sell to Russia and Spanish and Italian sellers could only sell to customers across the European Union. At the time, Turkey was an ideal market for AliExpress to enter because of its focus on export-led growth with high-quality goods and strong logistics infrastructure, as well as fast growing of e-commerce. As of today, tens of thousands of Turkish brands and SMEs are operating their stores on AliExpress' platform. Figure 3 presents AliExpress' milestones.

The SMEs that joined in the pilot launch,[4] which lasted until July 2019, experienced enviable success and rapid growth.[5] AliExpress displayed the success stories of some of these existing sellers on AliExpress' Global Seller page. Figure 4 presents some examples of success stories shared on AliExpress' Global Seller page in 2020. As can be seen, DeFacto's director of cross-border e-commerce states a 10-fold increase of the countries they can sell through AliExpress. Further, Elif Okur, the founder and owner of a small enterprise, shares her story of starting by sewing a tracksuit for herself to now selling on a global scale. The success of these sellers using AliExpress platform inspired other SMEs to join AliExpress. As a result, tens of thousands of other Turkish SMEs as well as top brands also opened their shops on AliExpress.[6] Correspondingly, the number of products listed in various categories increased to millions.

---

[3]Alexa rankings are a composite between "how many people are estimated to have visited the site" and "how many pages have been viewed" (from www.bigcommerce.com).

[4]"Launch" refers to AliExpress starting to accept seller applications from Turkey.

[5]The number of units sold of a particular product sold are displayed on AliExpress site. Hence, a potential seller can observe how many units sellers already sold via AliExpress.

[6]https://webrazzi.com/2019/07/10/aliexpress-turkiye-e-ihracat-bulusmalari/.

2010 – AliExpress officially launched: Chinese SMEs start using the platform. No localization, so all product information is in Chinese.
2011 – Product selection in AliExpress platform exceeded 10 million.
2012 – Chinese SMEs on AliExpress started primarily targeting Chinese consumers living overseas.
   – Russian language version launched.
2013 – Customers of AliExpress sellers span 200+ countries and regions.
2014 – Participated November 11 (11.11 Global Shopping Festival) festival, a shopping festival led by e-commerce platforms in China, for the first time, and generated over US$6.8 million sales.
2015 – Established local office in Russia.
2016 – English and other language versions of AliExpress became available.
   – On November 11 (11.11 Global Shopping Festival) order volume reached 35.78 million.
2017 – Global buyers exceeded 100 million.
   – Established local office in Spain, which manages AliExpress operations in Spain and Italy.
2018 – Global buyers exceeded 150 million.
   – AliExpress Turkey, Spain, Italy and Russia were launched (in December).
2019 – Launched "X-day delivery" service, ensuring delivery within a specific timeframe.
   – Established local office in Turkey.
2020 – Tenth anniversary of AliExpress.
   – Delivery service further enhanced. Launched "Three days local delivery" and "Ten days cross-border delivery" in Spain and France. On 11.11 Global Shopping Festival , the first package delivered within "half-day from purchase" in Spain.
2021 – AliExpress starts operations in France.

Figure 3. AliExpress' milestones.

Moreover, Figure 5 shows top selling categories by sellers via AliExpress Turkey to the rest of the world. Top selling categories differ from AliExpress Russia to AliExpress Spain to AliExpress Turkey since shipping products across borders face many rules and regulations. For example, electronics is not one of the top categories for sellers of AliExpress Turkey while it is one of the top categories for AliExpress Russia. Furthermore, Figure 6 demonstrates top markets for Turkish sellers. As can be seen in the figure, by listing their products on AliExpress, Turkish SMEs not only sell in Europe, but sell to countries as far as South Korea, Brazil, and the US.

Berkin Maden
Defacto Cross-Border E-Commerce Director

By increasing the number of countries we currently sell to 250 from 25 with Aliexpress, we took a big step in realizing our globalization strategies.

DeFacto

Dogukan & Berkant Gunes
Owner

AliExpress helps Turkish sellers to a better position by providing free training through AliExpress University. In this way, we achieved a considerable turnover by making sub-sales in a very short time.

SUNSPIRES Store

ELİF OKUR
MANUFACTURER & BRAND OWNER

I Sewed A Tracksuit For Myself, The Gates Of The World Are Opened. We currently both manufacture and market our products at a global level. Our orders have increased so much that we moved to a new workshop that will increase our production capacity.

Elif Okur Official Store

Figure 4.   Examples of success stories of Turkish sellers on AliExpress.

Figure 5. Top selling categories by Turkish sellers to the rest of the world.

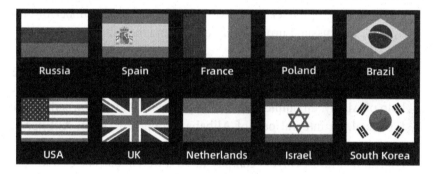

Figure 6. Top markets for Turkish sellers.

4. The Pillars of How AliExpress Helps Local Brands to Achieve Superior Performance

The success of AliExpress in helping local brands to achieve superior performance can be attributed to three areas: (i) lowering barriers to entry to potential sellers, (ii) leveraging its global infrastructure, and (iii) leveraging the local infrastructure.

4.1. *Lowering barriers to entry*

- *Fast, Easy, and Free Store Opening*: In addition to the fact that opening a store is free, there is no additional cost such as an annual store fee, subscription fee, or product listing fee. Standard company documents are required to open a store. Once a seller's application is approved by AliExpress, its store will be up and running within two business days.

- *Smaller Commission Means Bigger Margin*: The commission rates are below the industry average[7] as it varies between 5% and 8%, depending on the category.

4.2. *Advantages provided by the global infrastructure*

- *Integrated Sales Account Panel*: By only using a single integrated panel for using their AliExpress sales accounts (see Figure 7), merchants can sell to 150 million customers in more than 200 countries and regions. Top buyer markets, ranked by the total number of customers, are Russia, Europe, Middle East, and the Americas, especially the US and Brazil.
- *Easy Money Withdrawal*: Each seller is provided with an Alipay account immediately following the successful store opening. With the help of Alipay, an online and mobile payment platform owned by Ant Financial, an integral part of Alibaba Group ecosystem, AliExpress platform collects the money on behalf of the seller with strong risk control measures. Buyers can pay in 38 different currencies and payment methods. Upon successful delivery, the payment is transferred in USD to seller's Alipay account.
- *Seamless Localization*: The system provides auto-translation support in 18 languages for easy localization of the products and content provided by sellers. Also, end consumers buying at AliExpress and sellers (merchants) can communicate in their own languages on AliExpress website.
- *Low Return Rates*: AliExpress not only provides the necessary infrastructure to sellers to provide as much detail as possible in product detail pages, but also encourages and rewards sellers (e.g., by providing more marketing resources to them) to utilize the product detail page function. Also, buyers can contact and communicate with sellers

---

[7]Competitors such as hepsiburada.com in Turkey or mercadolibre.com in Spain sometimes charge commissions between 15% to 20%.

Figure 7. Sellers' integrated panel.

easily and ask questions before they purchase an item. Furthermore, since customers have to bear the delivery fee if they want to return an item they purchased, the return rates are very low compared to other platforms.

- *Advanced Logistics Solutions*: With AliExpress' global logistics infrastructure and know-how, orders are tracked by all parties online and real time, from seller's warehouse until it reaches to the buyer.

4.3. *Advantages provided by the local infrastructure*

- *Local Seller Support*: AliExpress provides local support for sellers. These subject matter expert agents can be reached via phone, email, and online chat during weekdays between 9:00 am and 6:00 pm. The agents not only answer questions, but also provide free consultancy to sellers on how to develop their stores.
- *AliExpress University Turkey*: AliExpress University Turkey offers online training courses for sellers who wish to learn more about stores operation, logistics, marketing and customer management. Content is fully localized and prepared by local team members and trainers who are carefully selected from successful sellers. Currently, the platform provides over 150 up-to-date videos and documents, blogs from sellers, and smart tools improving seller journey. See Figure 8 for a detailed story shared by a seller.
- *Seller Community*: To build and promote a seller community, AliExpress Turkey team introduced and actively promoted Dingtalk, an enterprise communication and collaboration platform developed by Alibaba Group. Thousands of local sellers use Dingtalk to communicate with AliExpress team and seller support, exchange opinions with other sellers, join special group campaigns, and attend trainings.
- *Local Logistics Solutions*: AliExpress logistics partners provide many services to sellers, such as pick up service from warehouse, basic fulfillment services, and warehouse operations.
- *Local Integration Partners*: Sellers can connect to AliExpress' back end via local integration service providers and manage many services online such as product listing, real time price and inventory updates, order management, and logistics.

"Hello, I am Vahap Karaağaç, a university student living in Izmir. I am one of the partners of EmiyandSamyStore. Undoubtedly, one of the most important days for EmilyandSamyStore was the day we joined the AliExpress platform. We immediately received our first order from the products we entered for trial purposes a few days after registration.

Although our first order was not very profitable for us as we entered with trial products, we successfully delivered our product to the customer with the idea of meeting the platform and keeping customer satisfaction at the forefront, and we received our first 5 stars. As a store, we move forward with the "Dropshipping" method. When choosing and listing products, we only have one question in mind: "Would I buy this?" And with this mentality, we made a lot of sales in a short time like 3 months and reached many of our goals.

Based on the experiences and successes we have gained in this short period of time, we wanted to mention for you the important points that you should pay attention to in order to be successful in AliExpress.

• Product Selection
• Store Decoration
• Customer Relationship
• Participation in Campaigns
• Product Listing and Marketing Settings
• Pricing

Product Selection:
Choosing the right product is very important for us. Because we have to be sure whether people buy a product or not. We make sure that almost every product we list is salable and interesting. It is very important that the product is a much needed product and that people can access this product with a single click without leaving their places. When choosing products, we need to be sure of the time we can supply and the durability of the product. Our first rule is that the product passes us first. In this way, we can see the product and intervene immediately in case of any problem. We make sure that the products are a need requirement and a solution product and "Can I buy this online?" We ask ourselves. In this way, it becomes easier to receive orders after our products are put on the market.

Figure 8.   A university student's journey to e-exporting shared on AliExpress University.

Store Decoration:

Before I opened my store, I was a graphic designer as a freelancer. That's why I tried to create a store decoration based on my old experiences and works. I wanted this decoration to be different and eye-catching from other stores. Accordingly, I recreated our store decoration with a work that took my days. The point where shop decoration is important: The customer visits your store after they have placed their first order from you and are satisfied. Decoration and design are very important here, because the customer should also arouse curiosity and desire. At this point, we created a visual for each product and each category and tried to attract the customer to the point we wanted. Order and meticulousness are important in decoration, because the customer would not be confused and it would be easier to find the desired product. In addition, the decoration will change the customer's perspective of the store and will provide a trust for the customer. Thanks to the decoration, the quality of the store will increase and the prejudice formed in the first place in the customer will be broken.

Customer Relationship:

The first rule, which is important in customer relations, can be considered as the golden rule of Turkish tradesmen: "The Customer is Always Right" rule ... If you communicate with the customer in a smooth, explanatory and courteous manner, your feedback will be high. As I mentioned at first, our first priority is the customer. We keep in touch with customers even after sales. When we see that the product is not delivered, the product is stuck somewhere, or when we encounter any problems, we contact the customer and explain the situation and explain the path they will follow in detail. Afterwards, we provide support to see if the product is delivered or not, and if there is anything we can do. We regularly check the status of our cargo daily. Because, as I mentioned above, it is easier for us to determine the condition of the product and whether there is something to be done.

Participation in Campaigns:

Campaigns are very important for us sellers. We get serious returns from every campaign we participate in. Thanks to these campaigns, we achieve high turnover and this campaign continues after the end of the period. AliExpress continuous campaigns to provide information about the Turkey team and nothing spectacular show us the path to be followed. Before the campaign period comes, we inform the sellers and show what we will do one by one. This is where the DingTalk application comes into play. In the DingTalk application, many groups have been established to support vendors and one-to-one support is provided from there. Necessary announcements are made every day and all questions are answered one by one. The team of Turkey as well as webinars by AliExpress campaign process gives information about the benefits of the campaign. They describe the promotions and actions that should be done in the campaign. In this way, it allows sellers to get out of the campaign process with a greater interaction.

Figure 8. (Continued)

Product Listing and Marketing Settings:
There are a few important points when listing the product. After making the necessary adjustments, the interaction of the product and the number of visitors increase more. Important points; product title, product images, marketing images, product information, correct category and description.

The product title is very important for the product to be found faster and to attract more attention. The title should contain information about the product. We try to keep the title as long as possible. Because the more details we give in the title, the more the product stands out. Product images show the quality of the product and attract the attention of the customer. In each of our products, we have 6 photos about the product and we make sure that these photos are in standard 1 : 1 sizes. Since potential customers cannot touch the product while shopping on e-commerce platforms, they want to see more details and learn more. If the product images and descriptions are sufficient in this regard, the rate of purchase of the product increases more.

Pricing:
When it comes to marketing settings, store promotions come into play. You can direct your store visitors to order with many methods such as displaying the product at a discount, special promotions for followers, store coupons, special offers, affiliates. To be more specific about affiliates, you specify a commission rate for the products you add to the program. AliExpress, on the other hand, advertises the product based on this rate and deducts from you in line with this rate per sale. In this way, a cooperation is made in the form of commission without paying large fees for advertising.

With store coupons and special offers, you can encourage visitors to buy the product more. Discounts and coupons you offer attract more customers' attention. In this way, you will double your sales.

Finally, I would like to tell you about the Freebies campaign. In this campaign, you present the product to customers on the home page with a free draw. Thus, your product is directly advertised and a serious influx of visitors occurs to your store. When you send the product to the winner in the campaign, the buyer also comments and scores the product, thus increasing the trust level of the customers for that product.

Before putting an end to my words, as a 20-year-old university student, I am taking firm and successful steps on this path. You have neither less nor more than me. I create my own brand value by e-export and continue to strive for my next goals. If I can achieve this, you can also succeed".

Vahap KARAĞAÇ — EmilyandSamy Store

Figure 8. (Continued)

5. A Guide to Effective Localization Process of Global Cross-Border E-Commerce Platforms

In this section, we present a guide to more effective localization that a B2C commerce platform can deploy when entering into new country markets. First, we elaborate on the various challenges such cross-border platforms face. We categorize various challenges during localization of a global platform such as AliExpress into three: "0 to 1", "1 to 10", "10 to 100 and beyond". Each of these levels comprises different tasks to achieve as well as their accompanying challenges, as depicted in Table 2. The main challenge transforms from operating in an ambiguous environment to sustaining growth as the number of sellers grow. At the same time, tasks range from "identifying potential partners in a local ecosystem" to "public relations activities such as promoting seller success stories". Now, we describe the step-by-step guide to effective localization of cross-border e-commerce platforms, also depicted in Figure 9.

5.1. *Define your principles*

First, it is vital to define your principles clearly and make sure that all team members understand, agree, and internalize. Here are the principles AliExpress set forth:

(a) *Customer first*: First, define the customer. Remember, your customers can be both sellers and end users/buyers. Next, learn who they are and what they want. Establish and keep the communication channels open and learn from them. Customers are best change agents and researchers that assist you.

(b) *Start small, scale fast*: No matter how big the brand or platform is globally, a realistic assessment is required in the local market. There is a quite high probability that the global best practices may not work locally. To find out what works and what does not, small and numerous trials are more valuable than assumptions. Teams should set key performance indicators (KPIs) for each task and assess the results after trials.

Table 2. Different challenges at different levels in localization of a global platform.

Level	Tasks	Main Challenge
0 to 1	• Set up the business (e.g., platform localization, payment, and logistics infrastructure setup) • Find out more about local sellers and understand their motivations • Find "friends and family" sellers from different profiles to test the entire customer journey • Identify potential partners (e.g., Integrators, logistics service providers, payment service providers, consultants, local trade associations) in the local ecosystem • Minimal marketing and public relations (PR)	Make numerous decisions in an uncertain setup
1 to 10	• Improve tasks in the business setup continuously • Analyze the satisfaction of goods and services as well as customer service • Attract more sellers with competitive commercial terms (e.g., low commission rate) and benefits • Test innovative methods to drive traffic and conversion • Commence segmenting sellers • Identify "star" products with high exposure and high traffic,* and sales growth • Test digital marketing (e.g., test various creative and text messages to understand how to maximize CTR) and PR • Increase awareness by attending and/or sponsoring selected conferences and/or various seller events (e.g., AliExpress e-commerce meetings organized in hotel conference halls**)	Balance hands on approach (talk to sellers in-person) and hone fighting skills, i.e., deep-dive into operations to understand problems and opportunities deeply without losing focus
10 to 100 and beyond	• Aggressive seller recruitment • Evaluate test results, find ways to boost growth • Iterate seller segmentation • PR activities such as promoting seller success stories	Achieve sustainable growth

Notes: *"Exposure" happens when the user/potential buyer sees the product, "traffic" happens when the user clicks to what s/he sees and goes to product detail. The exposure to traffic ratio is called "Click Through Rate" (CTR).

** See https://webrazzi.com/2019/07/10/aliexpress-turkiye-e-ihracat-bulusmalari/# for an example of such an event.

Figure 9.   A guide to effective localization process.

(c) *Scalability and sustainability*: Resources are always limited and should be directed to the most promising projects that is expected to have the highest impact. Even if a test or trial has successful outcomes, the feasibility for scaling needs to be conducted carefully. If the project (e.g., beginning operations in a different country) is not scalable or it is difficult to sustain, it is worth to consider exiting.

(d) *Stick to your strategy and embrace change*: This may sound contradictory, however it is necessary. Reviewing the principles set from time to time is required as market conditions change over time. In such cases, modifying the business and perhaps some of your principles is crucial for survival.

5.2   Understand the characteristics of your local ecosystem

After getting the principles right, the next level is to understand the market dynamics. There are various research methods that are being conducted by global companies when they do research on a country such as online research, paid phone consultations, and research reports. On the other hand, AliExpress conducts research differently: paid methods are mostly replaced by site visits, where team members travel to and spend significant time in a country, conduct field research, have one-on-one meetings with relevant people and, most importantly, experience the local social life and culture. In this regard, establishing local offices play a key role. As seen in Figure 3, AliExpress opened a local office in Russia in 2015 and another one in Spain in 2017, both several years before they started operations in those countries.

As research continues, team members summarize what they observe and experience in reports with many pictures and share what they learn with a larger community. In order to decipher the ecosystem more effectively, it is important to create a map and touch base with all stakeholders. Here are to name few:

Non-profit organizations
(1) Governmental organizations (e.g., trade ministries)
(2) Semi-governmental organizations (e.g., unions)
(3) Business associations (e.g., chambers of commerce)
(4) Industry-specific associations (e.g., Elektronik Ticaret Isletmeciler Dernegi — ETID[8])
(5) Universities.

Private organizations
(1) Competitors
(2) Supply chain parties (e.g., sellers, producers, retailers, distributors, and brand owners)
(3) Service providers (e.g., logistics companies, integrators, and agencies)
(4) Online and offline media (e.g., webrazzi.com in Turkey).

Other stakeholders
(1) Key opinion leaders (KOLs) (e.g., https://www.mserdark.com/)
(2) Industry professionals (e.g., president of ETID)
(3) Entrepreneurs (i.e., potential AliExpress sellers)
(4) Consumers.

This is obviously a long list and takes time. Therefore, desktop research is important to find out and reach relevant people before the site visits. However, to expedite this long and tedious process it is quite important to accelerate time to market. This brings us to the third step.

---

[8]An industry association of e-commerce businesses in Turkey. Please go to: www.etid.org.tr for more information.

5.3 Strengthen your front lines (hire local people; build bridges between your front line and headquarters; provide constant support)

Chinese companies have a good understanding and execution of martial arts in business life. In this context, overseas markets can be treated as the "Front Line", like in a battleground. Having the "right soldiers that fits the battle fought" will significantly contribute to the results. Therefore, hiring the right local people is the key to a successful localization, however, it is not enough. Just like the Chinese team members travel and conduct site visits to understand the local ecosystem and culture, local front-line team members also spend quality time in China headquarters to understand the company culture and ways of doing business. Successful localization is the outcome of a fruitful cooperation between teams from front line and headquarters.

5.4 Build and enhance your own ecosystem

However big is the local front-line team, it is never enough and never will be. It is also a fact that you cannot pile up people — against the scalability and sustainability principle. Still, you need human power to start a business quickly and grow it gradually. You need to revisit your earlier analysis of the ecosystem, interviews conducted, people met, and finally come up with potential partners that can be long-term allies to your cause. Recall the principle: Start small, scale fast. Smaller scale projects are a good way to test and build your local execution capability, as well as it will help you to assess the working relationship with your partner.

It is quite normal that you need to select some partners over others. This is a long-term play, so you need to keep all communication channels open. Further, it is highly likely that there is no suitable partner that fits your criteria. In such case, you need to rely on your local team to create partners that are designed specifically for your case. Creating partners can be achieved by encouraging entrepreneurs to setup a business that will serve your goals so that both you and they can grow together. This might be more costly in the short term, but this investment will pay off in the long run.

5.5 *Grow, analyze, and iterate — A never ending loop*

"Strategy grows from action" says an Alibaba proverb. Growth at all levels come with various challenges, which are quite difficult to anticipate, but also shape your strategy. Conducting periodic analyses of the business will help to align team members, fine tune strategy, assess priorities, and sustain focus. Continuous iteration and prioritization are necessary in the early phases during start-up period. Last, but not least, keep in mind the competitive landscape in terms of number and quality of existing e-commerce sites. The competitions' strengths in the local marketplace will have an influence on how fast you can grow and how frequently you analyze and iterate.

6. Concluding Remarks and Future Directions

Emerging SMEs, vying to leverage the spending power of the growing number of netizens in many parts of the world, can be better positioned when they deploy B2C cross-border e-commerce platforms. This is an area where more research needs to be done. For example, in many parts of the developing world, there is significant population that lives offline (e.g., elderly and poor), lacking access to the Internet or lacking the education and skills on how to use the Internet to make purchases. Hence, research needs to be done on how cross-border platforms such as AliExpress can overcome these digital divides so that the disenfranchised segments can join the digital commerce. In turn, AliExpress or Ctrip[9] and other companies venturing out to other fast emerging markets like Turkey should quickly figure out incorporating this into their growth strategies. According to an article published at the *Financial Times* in 2019, Trudy Dai, President of Alibaba's wholesale marketplaces division, noted that "From the very first day that Alibaba was founded, we had a 'global dream'", and AliExpress plans to roll out the service — which is called

---

[9]Turkey has a fast-growing tourism industry where countless B&Bs are vying to attract the right customers. According to United Nations World Tourism Organization's International Tourism Highlights Report for 2019, Turkey ranks sixth in the world for annual number of tourists (see https://www.e-unwto.org/doi/pdf/10.18111/9789284421152 for details).

"local to global" — in more countries after building up experience in the initial four counties, namely Russia, Spain, Italy, and Turkey. Ms. Dai also noted that "This strategy is intimately connected to Alibaba's broader globalization strategy". Not surprisingly, AliExpress started operations in France in 2021.

B2C cross-border online marketplace platforms such as AliExpress leverage technology and use cutting-edge knowledge management practices in order to create value for all stakeholders involved (Kumar 2018). Hence, another area for future research within this context could be to explore if and how the sellers in these cross-border platforms learn from their competitions as well as manage knowledge. Further, these e-commerce platforms must continuously balance efficiency and flexibility when operating in dynamic markets such as the fast-emerging Turkish market (Eisenhardt *et al.* 2010). Future studies must investigate optimal balancing strategies along with boundary conditions. Finally, vast amounts of data are accumulated on such e-commerce platforms, which is described as a vital source of superior performance, competitive advantage (Davenport and Harris 2017; Hagiu and Wright 2020), and of sustained innovation (Duan *et al.* 2020). Scholars should examine how these platforms ensure privacy and protection of such data, both of their sellers and of the end consumers.

In conclusion, in this chapter, by means of detailing AliExpress' story, we presented an example of a firm successfully localizing its platform and effectively using technological and other capabilities to enrich its customers' experience. In essence, this chapter also answers a call by Lemon and Verhoef (2016) for opening the black box of using technology in customer experience management. As noted earlier, these customers, i.e., sellers on AliExpress, are predominantly SMEs, whereby AliExpress enables their brands to reach to far corners of the world for mutual success.

References

Benmamoun, M., Alhor, H., Ascencio, C., and Sim, W. (2021). Social enterprises in electronic markets: Web localization or standardization, *Electronic Markets*, 31, 215–231.

Davenport, T. H. and Harris, J. G. (2017). *Competing on Analytics: The New Science of Winning*, Boston: Harvard Business School Press.

de la Cova, E. (2021). Language and brand: Problems for localization, *HERMES — Journal of Language and Communication in Business*, (61), 63–75. Retrieved from https://tidsskrift.dk/her/article/view/127925.

Duan, Y., Cao, G., and Edwards, J. S. (2020). Understanding the impact of business analytics on innovation, *European Journal of Operational Research*, 281(3), 673–686.

Eisenhardt, K. M., Furr, N. R., and Bingham, C. B. (2010). Microfoundations of performance: Balancing efficiency and flexibility in dynamic environments, *Organization Science*, 21(6), 1263–1273.

Hagiu, A. and Wright, J. (2020). When data creates competitive advantage, *Harvard Business Review*, 98(1), 94–101.

Kumar, V. (2018). Transformative marketing: The next 20 years, *Journal of Marketing*, 82(July), 1–12.

Lemon, K. N. and Verhoef, P. C. (2016). Understanding customer experience throughout the customer journey, *Journal of Marketing*, 80(November), 69–96.

Ramamurti, R. and Williamson, P. J. (2019). Rivalry between emerging-market MNEs and developed-country MNEs: Capability holes and the race to the future, *Business Horizons*, 62, 157–169.

Singh, N. (2011). *Localization Strategies for Global E-Business*, Cambridge: Cambridge University Press.

Tian, Y. and Stewart, C. (2006). History of e-commerce. In *Encyclopedia of E-Commerce, E-Government, and Mobile Commerce*, ed. Mehdi Khosrow-Pour, Pennsylvania: IGI Global, Chapter 90, pp. 659–564.

Zeng, M. (2018). *Smart Business: What Alibaba's Success Reveals about the Future of Strategy*, Boston, MA: Harvard Business Review Press.

Hierarchical Branding Strategy for New Product Launch: Evidence from China

Howard Pong Yuen Lam and Vincent Chi Wong

1. Introduction

When marketers develop a new product, they choose (or create) a brand name for it and expect that this name can increase the chances of success of the new product. Finding a name when introducing a product to China is more challenging than introducing it to most other countries because Chinese language has thousands of characters, each with many meanings and with pronunciations that vary from region to region (Fetscherin *et al.* 2012). As a result, marketers have to conduct rigorous marketing research on different names proposed by their creative agencies in China.

Thomas *et al.* (2004) suggest that a brand is a promise to consumers and that promise is delivered through source identifiers, the "five second sound bites" of a brand, and a strong identity must be protectable legally. They suggest a protectability continuum from the strongest to the weakest for a brand name to be: (1) arbitrary (or fanciful), (2) suggestive, (3) descriptive, and (4) generic. "Fanciful identifiers are the strongest and are the most easily protected against copycats. Examples include Clorox bleach, Pepsi Cola, and Kodak. These are invented words that have no other meaning. Arbitrary identifiers like Apple computers are in common linguistic use, but have nothing to do with the product it identifies. On the other hand, a suggestive identifier is one that implies the nature or characteristics of the product. Coppertone suggests that users of that suntan oil will have a coppery-toned tan. Suggestive identifiers are a good compromise between marketing and legal concerns. They communicate information to the customer about the nature of the product and are protectable against use by others. Descriptive identifiers express the function or characteristics of products. Example includes Superglue adhesive. These identifiers describe something about the product. They can't be protected against infringement unless they have become distinctive to the consuming public. A generic is exactly what it sounds like: the category name for a type of good and service. Such terms can never be protected legally" (Thomas *et al.* 2004).

Keller *et al.* (1998, p. 55) proposed that a "suggestive" brand name could convey information regarding a relevant attribute or benefit in a particular product context. They found support on the proposition that compared with a non-suggestive brand name (e.g., Emporium televisions), a brand name that explicitly conveyed a product benefit (e.g., Picture Perfect televisions) and produced greater recall of an advertised benefit claim that was consistent with the brand name's connotations.

For a new product, marketers must also determine a corporate branding strategy. For example, while P&G uses separate brand names without much reference to the corporate brand, Philips uses its corporate brand prominently, and Nestle uses its corporate name as an "endorsement" for its products (Berens *et al.* 2005, p. 35). An important managerial question involves what and how overall corporate branding and product branding strategy can help marketers increase the chance of success of a new product?

This chapter provides insights to marketers when answering the following questions. Should marketers in China follow suggestions of Zhang and Schmitt (2001) or Fetscherin *et al.* (2012) to create corporate name or product brand names from English to Chinese based on phonetic, semantic and phono-semantic methods? Alternatively, should marketers create names with suggestive meanings and if so, what should a name suggest? Should marketers use one name as both corporate name and product brand name or should they create two names with two different meanings for corporate name and product brand name, respectively? Is there a framework for marketers to follow when they develop brand names for launching new products in sequence and deciding on the appropriate corporate branding strategy for the new products? We first start with an overview of brand name translation methods.

2. Name Translation Methods

Whether a brand name is arbitrary, suggestive, descriptive, or generic in English, marketers and copywriters at creative agencies have to propose different names in the local language. In terms of translation methods, Zhang and Schmitt (2001) and Fetscherin *et al.* (2012) suggest three methods: phonetic, semantic, and phono-semantic. Therefore, certain product brand names may suggest meanings to consumers (semantic and phono-semantic), while others may not (phonetic).

Brand naming using a translation method is more challenging in logographic languages (e.g., Chinese), compared with phonographic languages (e.g., English) because the former languages feature looser correspondence between sound and meaning (Wu *et al.* 2019). Hence, Wu *et al.* (2019) propose to categorize brand name types for logographic languages into alphanumeric, phonetic, phono-semantic, or semantic. They use the Roman transliteration known as the Pin-yin system to present the Chinese brand names. Based on whether the Chinese name has similar sound as the English name (Yes, No) and whether the Chinese name has meaning or not, there are four different brand name types as shown in Table 1.

Table 1. Brand name types in logographic language.

		Meaning	
		No	Yes
Sound	No	Alphanumeric	Semantic
	Yes	Phonetic	Phono-semantic

Alphanumeric and phonetic brand name types are examples of arbitrary brand name mentioned earlier in this chapter. Semantic and phono-semantic brand name types are examples of suggestive or descriptive brand names, depending on the exact meaning of the name.

Wu *et al.* (2019) provide two examples of each brand name type in China, one for a multinational firm and the other for a domestic (Chinese) firm as follows:

Alphanumeric type (sound: no, meaning: no) includes 3M (a multinational from the US) and 360 (a popular internet security software brand in China).

Phonetic type (sound: yes, meaning: no) includes Motorola with Chinese name 摩托罗拉 (Pin-yin: Mou Tuo Luo La), which sounds similar to Motorola in English. Another example is Galanz (the largest microwave oven brand in China) with Chinese name 格兰仕 (Pin-yin: Ge Lan Shi), which sounds like "Galanz" in English.

Semantic type (sound: no, meaning: yes) includes Microsoft with Chinese name 微软 (Pin-yin: Wei Ruan), which means "tiny and soft" in Chinese. Lenovo's Chinese name (Pin-yin: Lian Xiang) means "association" in Chinese.

Phono-semantic (sound: yes, meaning: yes) includes Coca-Cola with Chinese name 可口可乐 (Pin-yin: Ke Kou Ke Le), which sounds like "Coca-Cola" and means "delicious happiness". Another example is E-land (a popular apparel brand in China) has Chinese name 衣恋 (Pin-yin: Yi Lian), which sounds like "E-Land" and means "loving clothes".

We have summarized these brand names from multinational firms and domestic (Chinese) firms in Tables 2 and 3.

Table 2.   Brand name types in logo-graphic language (multinational firms).

		Meaning	
		No	Yes
Sound	No	3M	Microsoft
	Yes	Motorola	Coca-Cola

Table 3. Brand name types in logographic language (domestic Chinese firms).

		Meaning	
		No	Yes
Sound	No	360	Lenovo
	Yes	Galanz	E-land

Wu *et al.* (2019) summarize the literature on these four brand name types. They gathered studies from primary marketing journals (e.g., *Journal of Marketing Research*, *Journal of Marketing*, and *Journal of Consumer Research*) and find that most of the studies are set in the US context and use lab experiments, with consumer as the unit of analysis and survey-based dependent measures as opposed to actual consumer choice. In contrast, the study of Wu *et al.* (2019) is set in the Chinese context, where they use observational field data with brand (e.g., Honda CR-V) as a unit of analysis and estimate a demand model based on unit sales.

Research on semantic brand names generally examines the relationship between the meaning of a brand name and consumers' brand perceptions and attitudes, mainly in phonographic language contexts. Research has shown that brand names that use familiar words or convey a product benefit (e.g., "Lifelong" brand luggage) enhance brand outcomes such as attitudes, perceptions, and recall (Keller *et al.* 1998; Lee *et al.* 2003; Peterson and Ross 1972).

Using automobile sales data from China and a discrete choice model for differentiated products, Wu *et al.* (2019) relate brand name types to demand, with evidence showing that Chinese consumers preferred vehicle models with semantic brand names (7.64% more sales than alphanumeric), but exhibited the least preference for phono-semantic names (4.92% lower sales than alphanumeric). In China, domestic firms benefited from semantic brand names, whereas foreign firms gained from using foreign-sounding brand names. Entry-level products performed better with semantic brand names, and high-end products excelled when they had foreign-sounding brand names. Thus, the four-way categorization of brand name types should help multinational firms and domestic (Chinese) firms understand and leverage the association between brand name types and consumer demand.

In another study, Gao *et al.* (2020) summarize prior research on brand name translation in international markets from 2001 to 2020 and develop a theoretical framework that integrates similarity, which focuses on how the translated brand name relates to the original brand name, and informativeness, which focuses on how the translated brand name reveals product content, to study the impact of brand name translations. Gao *et al.* (2020) analyzed Hollywood movies shown in China from 2011 to 2018. The results show that higher similarity leads to higher Chinese box office revenue, and this effect is stronger for movies that perform better in the home market (i.e., the United States). Also, when the translated title is more informative about the movie, the Chinese box office revenue increases. The informativeness effect is stronger for Hollywood movies with greater cultural gap in the Chinese market.

2.1. *Product branding strategy*

In this session, we use two examples to illustrate how marketers can create excellent Chinese brand names for a product with meaning. The first example is the translation of the English brand name of Coca-Cola to Chinese. The Chinese name of Coca-Cola 可口可乐 (Pin-yin: Ke Kou Ke Lei) is an excellent Chinese name with rich meaning, "delicious happiness". "可口 Ke Kou" means delicious and "可乐 Ke Lei" means happiness. Therefore, Coca-Cola has a suggestive name with meaning related to Coke's functional benefit (delicious) and emotional benefit (happiness).

Another example is from Lam *et al.* (2013). They showed how marketers might increase the chance of success for a new product launch. Since each newborn baby has a given name and a family name, Lam *et al.* (2013) suggest creating a "given name" and "family name" for the "new brand" of the new product. They reported the successful case of using "given brand name" and "family brand name" together — dual product branding strategy — by practitioners in China for the Minute Maid Orange Pulp juice drink launch. A suggestive given brand name helps consumers recall the key benefits and features of the new product. A suggestive family brand name communicates the benefits of the product category. A dual product branding strategy addresses the problem of using only one brand name for a new product launch. After the successful launch of the first new product with two names (given brand name + family brand name), marketers are able to launch other new products under "different" given brand names under the "same" family brand name in the future to meet different consumer needs. An analogue is that the first new-born baby now has younger brothers and sisters, and all of them have the same family name. Marketers may use the same family brand name to introduce different products to build scale for the brand, and are able to clearly differentiate the different product offerings under different given brand names under the same family brand name. When a company acquires a brand from another company, a marketer may position the acquired brand under the same family brand name only if the marketer had defined the business scope of the family brand broadly enough with a suggestive family brand name.

The case and research of Lam *et al.* (2013) provides empirical support for the success of using two names simultaneously in ascending order of abstraction for a new product. For Minute Maid, the Chinese given brand name has three Chinese characters 果粒橙 (Pin-yin: Guo Li Cheng). The meaning of these three Chinese characters is "Fruit Pulp Orange" and is suggestive of its key features and benefits. The Chinese family brand name of the new product is 美汁源 (Pin-yin: Mei Zhi Yuan) which means "Good Juice Source". It is also suggestive and positions Minute Maid as a juice-based wellness parent (family) brand. Lam *et al.* (2013) have described one Minute Maid case for their dual product branding strategy. They have not studied the interaction of corporate branding and product branding. Hence, there is a need to extend their work with empirical support.

2.2. *Corporate branding strategy*

Corporate branding is important for marketers in applying a product branding strategy (e.g., Ajami and Khambata 1991; Buil *et al.*, 2013; Knox 2004). "Consumers' cognitive associations for a company can be both a strategic asset and a source of sustainable competitive advantage. Because influencing these corporate associations is an important strategic task, marketers spend great sums of money each year on corporate advertising and related activities" (Brown and Dacin 1997, p. 68). Corporate brands are more likely than product brands to evoke cognitive associations of common products and their shared attributes or benefits, people and relationships, programs, and values (Keller and Lehmann 2006; Barich and Kotler 1991). A corporate brand provides consumers with expectations of what the corporation will deliver, and a "corporate brand promise" is similar to the "brand promise" of product brands (Argenti and Druckenmiller 2004, p. 368). The key question is what corporate association marketers should create for consumers. Before we provide an answer to this question, we describe the state of knowledge on this topic.

2.2.1. *Monolithic corporate branding strategy/Stand-alone corporate branding strategy*

Marketers can either choose corporate branding strategies in one extreme, that is, to use one corporate name for all products, or another extreme of using one brand name for each product. For example, General Electric mainly uses its corporate name as the brand name for all of its products. The advantage of this strategy is that the marketing investment to build the corporate brand image can benefit all products under the brand image. The disadvantage, however, is that it is difficult to create different brand images for different products. This corporate branding strategy is labeled as "monolithic corporate branding" (Berens *et al.* 2005; Laforet and Saunders 1994; Olins 1989). The other extreme is that marketers create one brand name for each product. The advantage is that marketers can build a clear image for each brand's target audience, whereas the disadvantage is that the brand building investment is high. Berens *et al.* (2005, p. 35) named this corporate branding strategy "stand-alone".

For example, P&G treats corporate name and product brand name as separate, and markets several products of a product category under one, two or more brand names, rather than creating one brand name for each product. For baby care, P&G has Pampers. For beauty and skin care, P&G has two key brands, SK-II and Olay. For hair care, P&G has four key brands, Head & Shoulders, Rejoice, Pantene, and Vidal Sassoon. P&G remains as a corporate brand name only. One major disadvantage of "stand-alone product" branding strategy is that marketers cannot achieve economies of scale in communication. For example, even though P&G is a sponsor of 2022 Winter Olympics in Beijing, P&G has to produce different commercials for different brands (Head and Shoulders, Gillette, etc.) to leverage the Olympics sponsorship and possibly spend significant amount of effort choosing the specific brands they will advertise more than others.

2.2.2. *Corporate brand name and product brand name —*
The same or different?

Some companies such as Coca-Cola and PepsiCo use the same name as company brand name and product brand name. So, the Coca-Cola Company uses the same name, Coca-Cola, as corporate name and as product brand name for cola beverages. The Coca-Cola Company, however, also has a range of products and brands covering many different beverages to meet different needs. The disadvantage of using Coca-Cola as the same name for company and for product of cola beverage is that it is not easy to create the right association for the brand as a company and as a product. Consumers have many different associations for Coca-Cola. As a company, Coca-Cola is friendly to the environment, cares for the community, is sportive and encourages global harmony with Olympics and World Cup sponsorships. As a product brand, Coca-Cola is refreshing, uplifting, and optimistic. These all have positive associations, but evoke different emotions in consumers.

In fact, when many companies grow from small companies into big multinational companies, marketers usually use the brand name for its key product as the corporate brand name. As marketing budget is limited when a company is small, marketers tend to put all the money on different activities into building one name to benefit both the product brand and corporate brand.

The problem arises when a company expands and thus, realizes that the same product brand name cannot be used for other categories. For example, marketers could not use Coca-Cola as the brand name to launch lemon-lime carbonated beverages, and so the Coca-Cola Company had to create the brand Sprite. Similarly, marketers of Coca-Cola China had to create Minute Maid as the family brand name for a juice-based wellness brand. As the associations of Coca-Cola did not fit the consumer healthy nutrition need of Minute Maid, marketers also could not use Coca-Cola Corporate name in a "monolithic" corporate branding strategy. Thus, companies can use "monolithic corporate" branding strategy for one consumer need, and "monolithic corporate" branding strategy for two or more consumer needs.

Marketers can use "monolithic corporate" branding strategy for meeting one consumer need such as "beauty and skin care". The advantage is that the company can focus its resources in building a consistent image for the company and also for all its products. For example, L'Oreal is a leading player in the beauty and skin care market and one of the several globally successful companies in consumer packaged goods industry (See Henderson and Johnson 2012, for a detailed study).

Marketers can also use "monolithic corporate" branding strategy for meeting two or more consumer needs. For example, the product line at Amway at first consisted of just one product, a biodegradable soap (Amway 2014). Subsequently, Amway expanded its business through direct selling business model to distribute its product in more countries, and also expanded its business by acquiring brands or creating brands for meeting different consumer needs. Amway's Nutrilite offers vitamin and dietary supplements for health care. Amway's Artistry offers products for beauty and skin care. However, for consumers and direct sellers who distribute Amway products, Amway has a heritage and image in kitchen cleaning detergent. So, marketers for Amway Artistry may find it difficult to compete with L'Oreal, because Amway has a heritage in detergent, while L'Oreal has a heritage in beauty and skin care. For consumers, it is harder to accept that a company with heritage in detergent can have expertise in producing products for taking care of soft and delicate skin of women. On the contrary, since its founding in 1909, L'Oreal has been pushing the boundaries of science to invent beauty and meet the aspirations of millions of women and men (Henderson and Johnson 2012).

We argue that if marketers are working for a fast moving consumer goods (FMCG) company such as P&G, marketers should evaluate whether or not they should mention the parent brand in product brand's communication. In fact, markets of SK-II do not mention P&G in their communications because P&G company brand may not have strong associations with high-end beauty products.

2.2.3. *Composite brand — Combination of two existing brand names*

Park *et al.* (1996) investigated the effectiveness of using a composite brand, a combination of two "existing" brand names, as the brand name for a new product. They offered a hypothetical example of the Godiva cake mix by Haagen-Dazs. Their studies reveal that by combining two brands with complementary attribute levels, a composite brand extension appears to have a better attribute profile when it consists of two complementary brands than when it consists of two highly favorable, but not complementary brands (Park *et al.* 1996, p. 453). Although marketers of two companies may negotiate joint promotions, it is not easy for marketers to create a joint venture between two companies for a brand launch (Spyropoulou *et al.* 2011). Furthermore, there are problems with the brand of a joint venture. The profit will be shared between Godiva and Haagen-Dazs. Hence, will there be enough incentive for each company to build (or support) distribution networks for the Godiva cake mix sold by Haagen-Dazs? In other words, for Godiva, the profit from Godiva's products is around two times that of the joint venture products of Godiva and Haazen-Dazs. The same situation applies to Haagen-Dazs' products vs. the joint venture products of Godiva and Haazen-Dazs. Hence, one question for us to ask is: Can marketers create a given name and a family name for a new product without the constraint of using an "existing" brand name of the marketer's own company and negotiate a deal to use another "existing" brand name from another company? If marketers could create names, what names should they create?

2.3. *Creation of suggestive corporate names*

In this section, we offer insights and recommendations pertinent to the question of what corporate brand names should suggest. Currently, marketers or company founders have at least three approaches to create suggestive corporate names.

2.3.1. *Suggestive corporate name — Product category*

Burger King, Pizza Hut, Kentucky Fried Chicken (KFC) are suggestive company names for their product offerings and "corporate ability" in different types of food. However, using products sold as company name might limit a company's growth. So, KFC's business suffered much more than McDonald's when there was bird-flu in Asia in 2003. Marketers at KFC also could not reposition KFC easily to offer Chinese food, and had to acquire other companies (Little Sheep in China), or created a new company. In 2005, KFC launched East Dawning 东方既白 (Pin-yin: Dong Fang Ji Bai) to offer Chinese food. East Dawning specializes in serving gourmet Jiangnan[1] cuisine such as Chinese style chicken soup or salty bean. The primary target groups are tourists and visitors in transit because the stores are predominantly located in bustling transportation hubs (Yum China 2020). Some Chinese food like chicken soup or salty bean can be found from the WeChat official account of East Dawning. In summary, these company names suggest to consumers what types of products these companies sell, not what consumer needs these companies will directly satisfy.

Managerial Take Aways

- While the use of suggestive product category names (chicken, pizza or burger) in the corporate name can help consumers know what the products they will have from the company, it limits what the company can offer in the product portfolio in the future.
- This naming approach is based on the product concept, not the marketing concept. Product concept assumes that consumers will buy product with a certain quality, performance or features (Kotler and Keller 2016, p. 43). Marketing concept focuses on what the consumers really need (high quality food delivered with excellent services in a restaurant), rather than the type of product (chicken, pizza or burger) (Kotler and Keller 2016, p. 43).

---

[1] Jiangnan is Pin-yin of the two Chinese characters 江南 which means southern part of the Yangtze river.

2.3.2. *Suggestive corporate name — Founders*

Many company founders use their own names to create company names. One key advantage is that the company can benefit from awareness and image of the founder. For example, Li Ning, a famous Chinese Olympics gold medalist, performed for several minutes in walking around the ceiling of the Bird Nest stadium before he lighted up the cauldron in the opening ceremony of Beijing 2008 Olympics. Li Ning's performance in Beijing Olympics is an extremely valuable event to build awareness of the corporate brand name of "Li Ning". For Adidas, an Olympics sponsor and competitor of "Li Ning" sports company, the appearance of Li Ning is a major ambush marketing event. That is, a company, often an event sponsor's competitor, attempts to deflect the audience's attention to itself and away from the sponsor and reduce the effectiveness of the sponsor's message while undermining the quality and value of the sponsorship opportunity that the event owner is selling (Meenaghan 1996). However, the major disadvantage of using company founder's name as company name is that the founder may get old, and the sportive image of "Li Ning" may deteriorate. Another disadvantage is that the name may suggest some meaning to consumers which the company may not want. Ning means "inactive" in Chinese, not "active".

Let us now consider how Li Ning could handle taking its brand abroad, especially to Western markets. They can use an approach similar to Lee Kum Kee. Lee Kum Kee was founded as an oyster source manufacturer over a century ago. The third generation leader, Mr. Lee Man Tat, set his eyes to make this sauce available to consumers globally. When doing so, the company had to change the brand to LKK so that consumers would not feel alienated with the full name. Following these footsteps, Li Ning can adopt "LN" or "LI-N" when entering into other countries.

We propose that LI-NING be shortened to LI-N instead of LN, because of several reasons. First, the current name is LI-NING, and so LI-N can keep the part about LI, the family name of many Chinese people. Second, LI-N is better than LI in helping consumers relate to the current company name of LI-NING. Third, legally, it is difficult to register a trademark of LI globally and stop all other companies to use LI. It should be easier to get trademark registration for LI-N as a short form for the current one of LI-NING. Lastly, when Chinese introduce themselves to foreigners, they first state their family name and then their given name. As it is difficult for foreigners to remember two names, Chinese mainly introduce the family name and give the initial of the given name. So, for "Li Ning", he can introduce himself to foreigners as having family name of LI and initial of N.

In the Western world, Ray Kroc, the key person behind the global success of McDonald's, also decided to use the family name of McDonald's brothers to expand McDonald's business globally. So, McDonald's can offer a range of products, and the name of McDonald's is less limiting than Burger King, Pizza Hut, or Kentucky Fried Chicken and more astute than Kroc Burgers. However, the Chinese company name of McDonald's may require more marketing investment to build than the Chinese company of "Burger King 汉堡王" which literally means "King of Burger". It is difficult for consumers to remember McDonald's company name, and the name may even create wrong consumer associations. For example, some Chinese consumers think the Chinese phonetic translation of McDonald's is "麦当奴" which means "Mc being slave". The right Chinese company name for McDonald's is "麦当劳" which means "Mc being labour". The confusion arises because the pronunciation of these two Chinese names are the same. These two meanings, right or wrong, however, have little to do with the four pillars for the success of McDonald's: QSCV, which stands for Quality, Service, Cleanliness and Value.

As the full name of McDonald's name is phonetic translation with Pin-yin of "Mai Dang Lao", Chinese has created a short name for it by simply using the first Chinese character of it with the sound of "Mai" and put the second character to be "Ji". About 100 years ago, when Chinese formed a new company, they might simply use their own personal name and added a Chinese character of "Ji" at the end. Ji is the Pin-yin for the Chinese character 记. Its meaning is similar to "entity" in English. So, Chinese may simply say "Mai Ji" 麦记. Hence, we have Lee Kum Kee with Chinese characters of 李錦記 and Pin-yin of "Li Jin Ji" because it was founded by a man, 李錦裳 (Pin-yin: Li Jin Shang). So, the company has the first two Chinese characters of this founder and the third Chinese character is Ji ("Kee" is the romanization of "Ji" in Guangdong accent).

While there are several reasons for the smaller success of Burger King relative to that for McDonald's and KFC in China, the Chinese name of Burger King 汉堡王 (Pin-yin: Han Bao Wang) is also a contributing factor for Burger King's smaller success: Hang Bao Wang has two meanings to Chinese, which may limit its appeal to Chinese consumers. First, "Hao Bao" means burger. So, it simply communicates to Chinese that Burger King offers burger. While dumplings are popular traditional food among Chinese, burger is not. Compare this to McDonald's in China: To succeed, McDonald's started offering food other than burger. Another problem with the Chinese name of Burger King is its third Chinese character which literally means "King". In Chinese culture, individuals (or other entities) are expected not to stand out too much from a crowd and become too individualistic. Chinese also are educated by their parents and teachers to be humble. So, by claiming itself being the "king" of Burger, Burger King in fact is not humble, and has set up very high expectation for its burger that it may fail to meet. Chinese would expect its burger to be significantly better than the burger from McDonald's. In reality, this is not the case.

English name	McDonald's	KFC	Burger King
Chinese name	麦当劳	肯德鸡	汉堡王
Pin-yin	Mai Dang Lao	Ken De Ji	Han Bao Wang
Meaning	Sounds like McDonald's	"Ken De" sounds like Kentucky. "Ji" is chicken in Chinese	"Han Bao" means burger. "Wang" means king
Translation approach	Phonetic	Phono-semantic	Phono-semantic
Positioning	American burger	Tasty chicken	King of burger
Appeal to Chinese	Average	Strong[*]	Below average

Note: [*] The Appeal to Chinese is explained in the paragraph under the table.

As can be seen in the table above, where we compare the three American QSR chains, of the three, KFC's Chinese name has the strongest appeal to Chinese consumers. First, traditionally, Chinese eat a lot of chicken. The time to get one kilogram of chicken meat from a chicken is less than that for getting one kilogram of beef, because it takes longer time for a cow to grow than for a chicken to grow. The cost per kilogram of chicken meat is less than that for beef. So, when budget is limited and Chinese need protein from meat, chicken meat is a lower cost option than beef. Also, the strong flavor of the KFC recipes can create the same taste even though the chicken are sourced locally and from different suppliers. KFC also does not require fresh chicken meat because Chinese cannot taste any difference from fresh chicken or frozen chickens with the strong flavoring of the KFC recipe. On the contrary, McDonald's and Burger King have to maintain its global standard for the beef. Hence, raw material cost is higher for McDonald's than for KFC. So, it is not surprising that KFC can operate profitable stores in many locations while McDonald's and Burger King cannot afford to continue paying even the rent. As a result, McDonald's and Burger King have primarily lost to KFC in China in terms of store opening. In summary, for the four Ps of Marketing (Product, Price, Place, Promotion), both McDonald's and Burger King has lost to KFC in product cost competitiveness (beef vs. chicken) and in terms of places (opening stores).

2.3.3. *Suggestive corporate name — Arbitrary*

The third approach for creating company name is that founders create names with arbitrary suggestive meanings. Some company examples include Alibaba, Amazon, Apple, Baidu, Facebook, Google, and Yahoo. For Baidu, its Chinese name is 百度 with Pin-yin of Baidu.

The name Baidu was inspired by a poem written more than 800 years ago during China's Song Dynasty. "The poem compares the search for a retreating beauty amid chaotic glamour with the search for one's dreams while confronted by life's many obstacles ... Hundreds and thousands of times, for her I searched in chaos/Suddenly, I turned by chance, to where the lights were waning, and there she stood". Baidu, whose literal meaning is "hundreds of times" represents a persistent search for the ideal (Baidu 2020).

2.3.4. *Corporate name — What should it suggest?*

Levitt (2006, p. 1) argues that companies should stop defining themselves by what they produced and instead reorient themselves toward customer needs: "sustained growth depends on how broadly you define your business — and how carefully you gauge your customers' needs.

Business will do better in the end if they concentrate on meeting customers' needs rather than on selling products. What business are you really in? Had US railroad executives seen themselves as being in the transportation business rather than the railroad business, they would have continued to grow. Hollywood defined its business in movie, when it was actually in the entertainment business".

In China, we can also find company with name which limits its scope of business. One example is Little Sheep (2020). It used product brand name of 小肥羊 (Pin-yin: Xiao Fei Yang), which literally means little fat sheep. While it can focus on its communication as an expert in offering hot pot with sheep meat, it also limits what it can offer.

Hence, we recommend that the company name should be suggestive of what business the company is in and what the company's mission is. Each successful company must have a purpose expressed in its mission, and the company's mission is relevant to customer, is not changed frequently, and represents "corporate ability". This can also remind executives to continue building business, which will help enhance the "corporate ability" in the chosen business definition and better satisfy customer needs. Focusing on the customer is also consistent with the "jobs to be done" concept: Marketers should develop purposeful brands where products can be "hired" by consumers to perform jobs consumers want to get done (Christensen *et al.* 2005). FedEx, for example, designed its service to perform the job of "I need to send this from here to there with perfect certainty as fast as possible" (Christensen *et al.* 2005, p. 1). "A clear purpose brand acts a two-sided compass: one side guides customers to the right products. The other guides your designers, marketers, and advertisers as they develop and market new and improved products" (Christensen *et al.* 2005, p. 1). We propose that marketers should apply these suggestions of Christensen *et al.* (2005) to "corporate brand name" rather than limiting these suggestions on "product brand name".

We could identify two companies, which have suggestive corporate names on the mission and purpose, namely, Microsoft and Netscape. "Microsoft" represents software for microcomputer. Another example is Netscape. Originally named Mosaic Communications Corporation, the venture was later re-named Netscape Communications Corporation by Andreeseen and Clark (Corts and Freier 2003, p. 2). Navigator, the company's browser, was a spectacular success, capturing more than 60% of the market less than two months after its release in December 1994 (Yoffie and Cusumano 1999, p. 8). Netscape as a company name is suggestive of the future landscape of "Net". Navigator is also a suggestive name for users. It enables them to navigate through the vast network of information on the Internet. When Microsoft launched its product to compete with Netscape's Navigator, Microsoft also used a suggestive name, Internet Explorer (IE), which simply helps users to "explore" the Internet.

In China, the use of Internet is mainly via mobile phones now. So, people communicate and get information through apps on their mobile phones, such as QQ or WeChat, instead of going through browsers on a PC. According to the April 2020 report of China Internet Network Information Center (CNNIC 2020), among people with Internet access, 99% of them go to the Internet via mobile phones, vs. only 35% via laptop computers and 43% via desktop computers. In China, similar to the rest of the world, there are two key operating systems: one for Mac OS (Safari browser) and one for Windows (IE browser). As Microsoft Windows operating system is allowed to be used in China for decades, many websites are designed to be compatible with Internet Explorer.

3. Hypotheses Development: Improving New Product Success by Choosing the Right Branding Strategy

In this chapter, we propose a hierarchical branding strategy with two names for one product, a product *given* name and a product *family* name, and to bind them together on the launch of a new product, and also use a suggestive *corporate* name as an abstract umbrella brand to increase the chance of new product success. The hierarchical branding strategy is based on the classic category-based processing model in social psychology domain.[2] According to Fiske *et al.* (1999), when people form impressions about a new target, they tend to first judge whether the target's attributes fit an established category. If people perceive a fit, a more

---

[2]Yeo and Park (2006, p. 272) summarized the key conceptual framework for a branding strategy based on the distinction between category-based and piecemeal processing and earlier work such as Fiske *et al.* (1999) and Fiske and Neuberg (1990).

category-based impression formation process will occur. Specifically, when a new product and the original parent brand are sufficiently similar, consumers view them as belonging to the same category and evaluate the new product on the basis of the favorableness of this category independently of its specific attributes (Yeo and Park 2006, p. 272). In the case of Minute Maid in China, the use of the same family name (Good Juice Source) for the launch of the first new product (Fruit Pulp Orange) and for the launch of another new product (Fruit Pulp Premium Milk) in effect helped consumers view the two products as belonging to the same category. The particular family name (Good Juice Source) also helped consumers view the two new products as coming from the same source and belonging to the same category. On the contrary, "when consumers perceive a lack of category fit, the extension is given smaller probabilities of success" (Yeo and Park, 2006, p. 272).

The actual challenges for practitioners have inspired us to propose that product *given* brand names, product *family* brand names and *corporate* names play different strategic roles. Marketers can create a suggestive product given brand name for product benefits, a suggestive product family brand name for category benefits and a suggestive corporate name for the business that the company is in that meets consumers' needs.

In China, family name is particularly important. When two Chinese have the same family name, they may feel emotionally connected as they believe that they have the same common ancestors hundreds of years ago. Hence, the suggestion that a corporate name and a family product name be used to convey certain aspects of a new product could resonate much more strongly in the eyes of Chinese consumers. In China, people are strongly devoted to their family names, while for the US or Australia, people may have adopted new names because whoever came to those lands had a new start, giving up their past lives along with their names.

Thus, while we have borrowed the notion of suggestiveness from Keller *et al.* (1998), our proposal is different from previous work conceptually. First, Keller *et al.* (1998, p. 55) propose that a "suggestive" brand name could convey information regarding a relevant attribute or benefit in a particular product context. We propose that we could have two "suggestive" names for a product, a given name and a family name. We also suggest strategic meaning for these two names, the suggestive given name should give meaning for product benefits, the suggestive family name should give meaning for the category benefits. Keller *et al.* (1998) did not study corporate branding and what corporate name should suggest. We extended their work and conducted a study to provide support that corporate name should also be suggestive. We recommend that the suggestive corporate name should give meaning for the business that the company is in that meets consumers' needs.

As it is also important for practitioners to have actionable guidelines on what is "new product success" and "goodness of name", we have developed two constructs. For "new product success", the six items are overall liking, purchase intention, purchase frequency, credibility, uniqueness, and relevancy. We recommend these items for the "new product success" construct because marketers often look at scores of these items to determine whether they can continue product development in a stage-gate process within an organization.[3] Marketers and research agencies have also used these items following the suggestions of Malhotra (2020, p. 341) and Lam *et al.* (2013, p. 587). Although marketers can create different names, they also need to know which one to use. So, we propose another construct, "goodness of name", with four items: overall liking of the product name, influence of the product name on the product image, the level of fit of the product name with the product description, and ease of remembering the product name. Marketers must assess the overall liking of the product name and need a name to enhance the product image that fits the product description. If consumers can easily remember a name, the marketing investment for building awareness of the name will be more efficient. These item measures are also general enough for marketers to use for different product categories.

For details on the research hypotheses, method, analysis and results for Two-Level Hierarchical Branding Strategy and Three-Level Hierarchical Branding Strategy, please see Appendix I of this chapter.

Marketers may increase the chance of success for a new product launch by adopting a hierarchical branding strategy with ascending order of abstraction with three names with different suggestive meanings. Below is a summary of our specific suggestions to managers:

---

[3]For details, please refer to Aaker *et al.* (2019, p. 217) and Hair *et al.* (2021, p. 200).

Managerial Take Aways

- Use a suggestive given name for the new product that helps consumers recall the key benefits and features of the new product.
- Use a suggestive family name for the new product that communicates the benefits of the product category. By giving the new product a suggestive corporate name, new product success can be further enhanced if the corporate name is suggestive of the key business that the corporation is in and the consumer needs it seeks to satisfy.
- In terms of measures, there are guidelines on what is "new product success" and "goodness of name".

3.1. Discussion

There are three key theoretical contributions of our study. One is that the use of a hierarchy of brand names constitutes a new framework of branding for new product launches, providing a consumer-based perspective on new product management strategies. Specifically, the present research suggests that a hierarchy of names provides consumers with additional cognitive cues in tracing the desirable characteristics of an established brand. Second, the new framework is strategic and considers a long-term perspective, as the focus is not on the success of launching one single product, but on the branding strategy for successfully creating an umbrella brand with different products with different given names in sequence. The creation of two names for a new product is similar to what parents will create for their newborn baby, a given name and a family name. The family name reminds consumers of the linkage between the established product/brand equity and the newly launched product (and is also important in Chinese markets), whereas the given name suggests the value/function conveyed by the new product. Third, prior research has suggested that products are akin to humans (Aaker 1997; Aggarwal and McGill 2012; Jordan 2002; Rojas-Méndez *et al.* 2013). Consumers' perceived product personalities play an essential role in determining product evaluation (Aggarwal and McGill 2007), loyalty (Chandler and Schwarz 2010), and risk taking (Kim and McGill 2011). The current research further extends the research of product anthropomorphism to the study of given/family names of brands. With the introduction of given/family names to the product anthropomorphism theory, we are more able to visualize a brand or product with human-like characteristics. In turn, this helps us to advance our knowledge of understanding the emotional bonds between brands and consumers.

4. Conclusion and Future Research

We extend the work of Keller *et al.* (1998) and Lam *et al.* (2013) by proposing and empirically demonstrating a three-level hierarchical branding strategy for new product launch, which is characterized by the binding of a suggestive given name and a suggestive family name for a new product. Besides, by putting the new product under a suggestive corporate name, marketers can further enhance new product success if the corporate name is suggestive of the key business that the corporation is in and the consumer needs it seeks to satisfy, especially in China. Because the actual name used is highly important, marketers should treat this factor seriously and ask creative agencies to propose different names with different levels of abstraction. Marketers do not want to use a suggestive name with negative connotations.

A. Appendix I — Research Hypotheses, Method, and Results

A.1. *Two-level hierarchical branding strategy*

The suggestive product *given* brand name helps consumers recall the brand, its benefits or its points of difference. The suggestive product *family* brand name enables marketers to gradually build the parent brand to be an umbrella brand covering the key benefits of the product category; thus, the two names for the product are complementary. By printing *"product given name by product family name"* on the front packaging label, marketers can build awareness of the product family name. Marketers can establish ownership of the "category" via a suggestive family brand name. When the awareness of the first product's given name and family name are at a similar level, marketers can use the same family name to launch a second new product with a second given name, and so on. These steps form the core essence of the two-level hierarchical branding strategy.

H1: A new product with "one suggestive brand name" will receive more positive responses compared to that with "one non-suggestive brand name".

Following H1 and the successful case of Minute Maid in China:

H2: A new product with "one suggestive given brand name plus one suggestive family brand name" will receive more positive responses compared to that with "one non-suggestive brand name".

Furthermore, we hypothesize that:

H3: A new product with "one suggestive given brand name plus one suggestive family brand name" will receive more positive responses compared to that with "one suggestive given brand name plus one non-suggestive family brand name".

A.2. *Three-level hierarchical branding strategy*

For corporate branding strategies, we empirically tested the use of suggestive or non-suggestive corporate names and their combination with a product given brand name and product family brand name.

H4: A new product with "a suggestive corporate name" will receive more positive responses compared to that with "a non-suggestive corporate name".

H5: A new product with "a suggestive corporate name and another suggestive product family brand name" will receive more positive responses compared to that with a non-suggestive name as both "corporate name and product family brand name".

Furthermore, we propose that using one name as both the corporate name and the product family brand name (e.g., Coca-Cola) is not ideal for communication and therefore may affect consumers' responses. Thus:

H6: A new product with "a suggestive corporate name and another suggestive product family name" will receive more positive responses compared to that with a suggestive name as both "corporate name and product family brand name".

Although the naming strategy of Coca-Cola as both a corporate name and a product family brand name is not ideal for communication, we hypothesize that a suggestive name will nevertheless enable the concept to be associated with more positive responses compared with a "non-suggestive" name as both a corporate name and a product family brand name. Thus:

H7: A new product with a suggestive name as both the "corporate name and the product family brand name" will receive more positive responses compared to that with a non-suggestive name as both the "corporate name and the product family brand name".

Because the suggestiveness of a brand name can produce greater recall of the claimed benefits of the product, which is consistent with the brand name's connotations (Keller *et al.* 1998), we further hypothesize that:

H8: The ease of remembering the product name will be significantly correlated with participants' responses to a new product.

A.3. *Method*

We followed Lam *et al.* (2013) and used a concept test to quantitatively measure consumers' reaction to the same product with different corporate and product brand names using an experimental approach. In terms of product categories, we followed Keller and Aaker (1992) and Lam *et al.* (2013) and chose snacks (i.e., potato chips) because respondents are expected to have purchase and usage experience. For the Chinese family brand names of the stimuli, we followed the approach of Zhang and

Schmitt (2001, p. 317) and Lam *et al.* (2013), using fictitious names to minimize any familiarity and prior knowledge factors. The Chinese stimulus names were presented with Chinese characters in the experiment. We used the same procedure as Zhang and Schmitt (2001) and Lam *et al.* (2013), informing all of the respondents that the study involved brand names and that they would be given brand names that might be used for actual products in the future and that might appear on product packaging and promotional materials. We also emphasized the Chinese name in larger, bold typeface in the experimental instrument (Zhang and Schmitt 2001; Lam *et al.* 2013).

We followed Lam *et al.* (2013) and used the same new product concept (Appendix II). While Lam *et al.* (2013) focused on a two-level hierarchical branding strategy, our experiment extended this strategy to a three-level hierarchical structure. There are five product concepts (Table 4) for the different branding strategies. We develop family names with a higher level of abstraction than given names. We have two suggestive corporate brand names (i.e., A and C) for the branding strategy of using a

Table 4. Five product concepts in study 1.

Concept	A	B	C	D	E
Number of names	Two names	Two names	Two names	One name	One name
Parent brand name	Suggestive	Non-suggestive	Suggestive	Suggestive	Non-suggestive
Sub-brand name	Suggestive	Suggestive	Suggestive		
Parent brand name — English	Xiang Su	Ke Li	Xiang Su	Potato "zero" chip	Ke Li
Parent brand name — Chinese	香酥	克立	香酥	马"零"薯	克立
Sub-brand name — English	Potato "Zero" Chip	Potato "Zero" Chip	"Zero" Potato Chip		
Sub-brand name — Chinese	马"零"薯	马"零"薯	"零"薯片		

suggestive given product brand name and a suggestive parent product brand name so as to rule out the possible interpretation that the findings were due to the uniqueness of a name.

To test our hypotheses, we conducted two experiments with nested within-designs. Study 1 tested our hypotheses concerning a two-level hierarchical branding strategy (family, given brand names) for new products (H1–H3), while study 2 tested our hypotheses for a three-level hierarchical branding strategy (family, given brand names, and corporate name; H4–H8). A global research agency conducted the research fieldwork in Shanghai, China and provided statistical significance tests at the 95% confidence level. The agency conducted online interviews with a total of 1,000 respondents (50% male and 50% female, average age of 29) across two studies.

A.3.1. *Study 1*

Study 1 had a 2 (number of product names: one vs. two) × 2 (name suggestiveness: suggestive vs. non-suggestive) nested-within design. The design generated five branding concepts as shown in Table 4: concept A (suggestive family/suggestive given brand names), B (non-suggestive family/suggestive given names), C (suggestive family/suggestive given names), D (one suggestive name), and E (one non-suggestive name). We counterbalanced the order of presenting the five concepts to rule out any recency/primacy effect(s).

A.3.1.1. Study 1 — Procedure and measures

A global research agency conducted 500 online interviews (50% female and 50% male, average age of 29) in China. All respondents must have consumed potato chips in the previous three months. We presented five new product concepts to each participant and measured their responses with regard to their overall liking and purchase intention on each product concept. Consistent with the previous literature (e.g., Fock *et al.* 2011), we asked participants to rate their purchase intentions using two items: *very likely/very unlikely* (7-point) and *purchase frequency*. We asked participants to note the number of purchases of the presented product out of ten potato chip purchases and transformed the purchase frequency (10-point) linearly into a 7-point scale. We then combined the two items to generate a purchase intention index ($\alpha = 0.71$). We used a single item to capture overall liking: *like a lot/dislike a lot* (7-point) (Hoek *et al.* 2013). Based on Bergkvist and Rossiter's (2007) recent research, for constructs in marketing that consist of a concrete singular object (i.e., attitude/liking of ads or brands), a single-item measure should be used to maximize the predictive validity.

A.3.1.2. Study 1 — Results of the responses to a new product

The results of a repeated-measure ANOVA revealed a significant difference between participants' purchase intentions regarding the new product for the five different concepts, $F(4,1996) = 39.79$, $p < 0.001$. To reveal the nature of the difference, we conducted a follow-up contrast. Consistent with the literature and the prediction in H1, participants showed significantly higher intentions to purchase the product for concept D ($M = 4.77$, $SD = 1.21$) than for concept E ($M = 4.24$, $SD = 1.36$, $F(1, 1996) = 118.60$, $p < 0.001$). Participants' purchase intention for concept A ($M = 4.67$, $SD = 1.24$) was significantly higher than that for both concepts E ($M = 4.24$, $SD = 1.36$, $F(1, 1996) = 82.95$, $p < 0.001$) and B ($M = 4.42$, $SD = 1.30$, $F(1, 1996) = 25.68$, $p < 0.001$), empirically supporting H2 and H3. The same pattern of significant results was obtained by replacing concept A with concept C. The statistical result concerning overall liking replicated that concerning purchase intention.

A.3.2. Study 2

While Study 1 focused on a two-level hierarchical branding strategy, Study 2 extended this strategy to a three-level hierarchical structure. That is, Study 2 aimed to test the use of suggestive or non-suggestive corporate brand names, family brand names and given brand names. Study 2 differed from Study 1 in the following aspects. First, Study 2 took corporate brand names into consideration and tested the proposed multiple-name branding strategy in a broader context. Second, based on the results of Study 1, Study 2 kept given brand names constant as suggestive and focused on the additional value of corporate brand names. Third, Study 2 used the measurement approach of a global marketing research agency to enhance the linkage between theory and practice.

Study 2 employed a 2 (number of product names: two vs. three names) × 2 (name suggestiveness: suggestive vs. non-suggestive) nested within-design. The design generated five branding concepts, as shown in Table 5: concept P (suggestive corporate name/suggestive product family brand name/suggestive product given brand name), Q (the same structure as P, but a different corporate name), R (non-suggestive corporate name/suggestive family name/suggestive given name), S (a suggestive name as both corporate and family names/suggestive given name), and T (a non-suggestive name as both corporate and family names/suggestive given name). We developed corporate names with a higher level of abstraction than family names and given names.

A.3.2.1. Study 2 — Procedure and measures

The same global research agency conducted another 500 online interviews (50% female and 50% male, mean age of 29) in China. We presented five new product concepts to each participant with their order counterbalanced. Following the modern practical marketing research, we selected six items that are commonly used by marketing managers (overall liking, purchase intention, purchase frequency, credibility, uniqueness, and relevancy) to capture participants' responses towards the new product. An overall "new product success" index was generated by averaging these six items (Zhang and Schmitt 2001; $\alpha = 0.92$). Finally, following Hong and Sternthal's (2010) research on processing fluency, we used a single item, *very easy/very difficult* (7-point), to measure the ease with which participants could remember the product name.

A.3.2.2. Study 2 — Results

The results of a repeated-measure ANOVA revealed a significant difference for the five concepts in terms of "new product success", $F(4,1996) = 2.91$, $p < 0.05$. Consistent with the predictions in H4, H5, and H6, the results of *a priori* contrasts showed that concept P ($M = 5.53$, $SD = 1.14$)

Table 5. Five corporate name and product brand name concepts in study 2.

Concept	P	Q	R	S	T
Corporate brand name	Suggestive	Suggestive	Non-suggestive	Suggestive	Non-suggestive
Corporate brand name — English	Quality health source	Health happy source	Yi Er Na	Quality health source	Yi Er Na
Corporate brand name — Chinese	优健源	健乐源	伊尔纳	优健源	伊尔纳
Product family brand name	Suggestive	Suggestive	Suggestive	Suggestive	Non-suggestive
Product family brand name — English	Xiang Su	Xiang Su	Xiang Su	Quality health source	Yi Er Na
Product family brand name — Meaning	Scented crispy	Scented crispy	Scented crispy	Quality health source	*No meaning*
Product family brand name — Chinese	香酥	香酥	香酥	优健源	伊尔纳
Product given name	Suggestive	Suggestive	Suggestive	Suggestive	Suggestive
Product given name — English	Potato "Zero" Chip	Potato "Zero" Chip	Potato "Zero" Chip	Potato "Zero" Chip	Potato "Zero" Chip
Product given name — Chinese	马"零"薯	马"零"薯	马"零"薯	马"零"薯	马"零"薯

received a significantly higher score in terms of "new product success" than that of concepts R ($M = 5.48$, $SD = 1.13$, $F(1,1996) = 4.93$, $p < 0.05$), T ($M = 5.43$, $SD = 1.16$, $F(1,1996) = 17.88$, $p < 0.001$) and S ($M = 5.49$, $SD = 1.06$, $F(1,1996) = 4.13$, $p < 0.05$). The same pattern of significant results was found when replacing concept P with concept Q in the analysis. Furthermore, concept S scored higher than T ($F(1,1996) = 6.00$, $p < 0.05$), providing empirical support for H7. Finally, a regression analysis showed that the new product success index can be well predicted by the ease with which participants could remember the product concept on a significant level ($t = 19.60$, $p < 0.001$), with a large explanation power ($R^2 = 0.44$; Cohen 1992). These results lend support to our prediction in H8.

Our research has several limitations. We have only focused on the product concept test before a product is launched on the market. Although this is an important early stage in product qualification within a stage-gate process, we have not conducted research on the product and usage stages or other later stages. In terms of product categories, we have only focused on potato chips within the snack food category out of many fast-moving consumer goods. We hope that this chapter encourages more researchers to test suggestive names in product concept tests and report their findings. Our research findings may not be applicable to industrial products when buyers place more importance on functional attributes than on the suggestiveness of a brand name.

A. Appendix II — New Product Concept in English

After working for a long time, you need some rest.
The new potato chip is crispy and delicious, but it does not contain any fat and salt (0% fat, 0% salt).
It is produced by a patented baking process. Without adding any oil, it nevertheless has a crispy texture. It also has specially added minerals that are essential for the human body and give it a delicious, slightly salty taste.
Try the new [Branding option] now.
Corporate Brand Name: [Branding option]
Family Product Brand Name: [Branding option]

Given Product Brand Name: [Branding option]
Product: Potato Chips
Weight: 50 g
Price: RMB3

References

Aaker, J. L. (1997). Dimensions of brand personality, *Journal of Marketing Research*, 34(3), 347–356.

Aaker, D. A., Kumar, V., Leone, R. P., and Day, G. S. (2019). *Marketing Research, Adaption of Marketing Research*, 11th ed., New Delhi: Wiley.

Aggarwal, P. and McGill, A. L. (2007). Is that car smiling at me? Schema congruity as a basis for evaluating anthropomorphized products, *Journal of Consumer Research*, 34(4), 468–479.

Aggarwal, P. and McGill, A. L. (2012). When brands seem human, do humans act like brands? Automatic behavioral priming effects of brand anthropomorphism, *Journal of Consumer Research*, 39(2), 307–323.

Ajami, R. A. and Khambata, D. (1991). Global strategic alliances: The new transnationals, *Journal of Global Marketing*, 5(1–2), 55–69.

Argenti, P. A. and Druckenmiller, B. (2004). Reputation and the corporate brand, *Corporate Reputation Review*, 6(4), 368–374.

Amway (2014). http://www.amway.com/about-amway/our-company/heritage/history-timeline (accessed on July 5, 2014).

Barich, H. and Kotler, P. (1991), A framework for image management, *MIT Sloan Management Review*, 32(4), 94–104.

Berens, G., van Riel, C. B. M., and van Bruggen, H. G. (2005). Corporate associations and consumer product responses: The moderating role of corporate brand dominance, *Journal of Marketing*, 69(3), 35–48.

Bergkvist, L. and Rossiter, J. R. (2007). The predictive validity of multiple-item versus single-item measures of the same constructs, *Journal of Marketing Research*, 44(2), 175–184.

Baidu (2020). http://ir.baidu.com/company-overview (accessed on November 10, 2020).

Brown, T. J. and Dacin, P. A. (1997). The company and the product: Corporate association and consumer product responses, *Journal of Marketing*, 61(1), 68–84.

Buil, I., Martínez, E., and de Chernatony, L. (2013), The influence of brand equity on consumer responses, *Journal of Consumer Marketing*, 30(1), 62–74.

Chandler, J. and Schwarz, N. (2010). Use does not wear ragged the fabric of friendship: Thinking of objects as alive makes people less willing to replace them, *Journal of Consumer Psychology*, 20(2), 138–145.

Christensen, C. M., Cook, S., and Hall, T. (2005), Marketing malpractice, the cause and the cure, *Harvard Business Review*, 83(12), 74–83.

CNNIC (2020). https://www.cnnic.net.cn/hlwfzyj/hlwxzbg/hlwtjbg/202004/P020200428596599037028.pdf (accessed on November 10, 2020).

Cohen, J. (1992). A power primer, *Psychological Bulletin*, 112(1), 155–159.

Corts, K. and Freier, D. (2003). Brief History of the Browser Wars, Harvard Business School Case, 9-703-571, June 9, 2003.

Fetscherin, M., Alon, I., Littrell, R., and Chan, A. (2012). In China? Pick your brand name carefully, *Harvard Business Review*, 90(9), 26.

Fiske, S. T. and Neuberg, S. L. (1990). A continuum of impression formation, from category-based to individuating processes: Influences of information and motivation on attention and interpretation. In *Advances in Experimental Social Psychology*, ed. M. Zanna, Vol. 23, pp. 1–74. San Diego, CA: Academic Press.

Fiske, S. T., Lin M., and Neuberg, S. L. (1999). The continuum model: Ten years later. In *Dual-Process Theories in Social Psychology*, eds. S. Chaiken and Y. Trope, pp. 231–254. New York: Guildford.

Fock, H., Chan, A. K., and Yan, D. (2011), Member-organization connection impacts in affinity marketing, *Journal of Business Research*, 64(7), 672–679.

Gao, W., Ji, L., Liu, Y., and Sun, Q. (2020). Branding cultural products in international markets: A study of Hollywood movies in China, *Journal of Marketing*, 84(3), 86–105.

Hair, J. F., Ortinau, D. J., and Harrison, D. E. (2021). *Essentials of Marketing Research*, New York: McGraw Hill.

Henderson, R. M. and Johnson, R. (2012). L'Oreal: Global brand, local knowledge, *Harvard Business School*, 9, 311–118.

Hoek, A. C., Elzerman, J. E., Hageman, R., Kok, F. J., Luning, P. A., and Graaf, C. D. (2013). Are meat substitutes liked better over time? A repeated in-home use test with meat substitutes or meat in meals, *Food Quality and Preference*, 28(1), 253–263.

Hong, J. and Sternthal, B. (2010). The effects of consumer prior knowledge and processing strategies on judgments, *Journal of Marketing Research*, 47(2), 301–11.

Jordan, P. W. (2002). *The Personalities of Products. Pleasure with Products: Beyond Usability*, London: CRC Press, pp. 19–47.

Keller, K. L. and Aaker, D. A. (1992). The effects of sequential introduction of brand extensions, *Journal of Marketing Research*, 24(1), 35–50.

Keller, K. L., Heckler, S. E., and Houston, M. J. (1998). The effects of brand name suggestiveness on advertising recall, *Journal of Marketing*, 62(1), 48–57.

Keller, K. L. and Lehmann, D. R. (2006). Brands and branding: Research findings and future priorities, *Marketing Science*, 25(6), 740–759.

Kotler, P. and Keller, K. L. (2016). *Marketing Management*, 15th ed., New York: Pearson.

Kim, S. and McGill, A. L. (2011). Gaming with Mr. Slot or gaming the slot machine? Power, anthropomorphism, and risk perception, *Journal of Consumer Research*, 38(1), 94–107.

Knox S. (2004). Positioning and branding your organisation, *Journal of Product and Brand Management*, 13(2), 105–111.

Levitt, T. (2006). What business are you in? Classic advice from Theodore Levitt, *Harvard Business Review*, 84(10), 126.

Laforet, S. and Saunders, J. (1994). Managing brand portfolios: How the leaders do it, *Journal of Advertising Research*, 34(5), 64–76.

Lam, P. Y., Chan, A., Gopaoco, H., Oh, K., and So, T. H. (2013). Dual branding strategy for a successful new product launch in China, *Business Horizons*, 56(5), 583–589.

Lee, Y. H. and Ang, S. H. (2003). Interference of picture and brand name in a multiple linkage ad context, *Marketing Letters*, 14(4), 273–288.

Little Sheep (2020). www.littlesheep.com (accessed on November 7, 2020).

Malhotra, N. K. (2020). *Marketing Research: An Applied Orientation*: Global edition (7th ed.), New Jersey: Prentice Hall.

Meenaghan, T. (1996). Ambush marketing — A threat to corporate sponsorship, *Sloan Management Review*, Fall, 38(1), 103–113.

Olins, W. (1989). Corporate identity: Making business strategy visible through design. London: Thames and Hudson.

Park, C. W., Jun, S. Y., and Shocker, A. D. (1996). Composite branding alliances: An investigation of extension and feedback effects, *Journal of Marketing Research*, 33(4), 453–466.

Peterson, Robert A. and Ross, I. (1972). How to name new brands, *Journal of Advertising Research*, 12(6), 29–34.

Rojas-Méndez, J. I., Papadopoulos, N., and Murphy, S. A. (2013). Measuring and positioning nation brands: A comparative brand personality approach, *Corporate Reputation Review*, 16(1), 48–65.

Spyropoulou, S., Skarmeas, D., and Katsikeas, C. S. (2011). An examination of branding advantage in export ventures, *European Journal of Marketing*, 45(6), 910–935.

Thomas, L. M. and Murry, N. M. (2004). Avoiding identity crisis, *Marketing Management*, 13(3), 44–45. We have added citation and a few paragraphs into the article.

Wu, F., Sun, Q., Grewal, R., and Li, S. (2019). Brand name types and consumer demand: Evidence from China's automobile market, *Journal of Marketing Research*, 56(I), 158–175.

Yeo, J. and Park, J. (2006). Effects of parent-extension similarity and self-regulatory focus on evaluations of brand extensions, *Journal of Consumer Psychology*, 16(3), 272–282.

Yoffie, D. B. and Cusumano, M. A. (1999). Building a company on Internet time: Lessons from Netscape, *California Management Review*, 41(3), Spring 1999.

Yum China (2020). http://www.yumchina.com/brand (accessed on November 7, 2020).

Zhang, S. and Schmitt, B. H. (2001). Creating local brands in multilingual international markets, *Journal of Marketing Research*, 38(3), 313–325.

© 2022 World Scientific Publishing Company
https://doi.org/10.1142/9789811249631_0006

Corporate Branding Strategy for New Companies in China: Lessons Learned from GoGoVan and LaLaMove

Howard Pong Yuen Lam and Shiyu (Tracy) Lu

1. Introduction

When entrepreneurs have a new business idea for an innovative good or service, they usually found a new company and create a company name to pursue the opportunity. They want their companies and offerings of products to be appealing to customers. Therefore, they make several key decisions on company and product names that have long-term implications. First, should the company name and the product/service brand name be the same? Second, should the company name suggest a meaning? If so, what meaning should the name suggest? In this chapter, we review literature and then summarize the key lessons learned from the company names of two startup companies, GoGoVan and LaLaMove. Subsequently, we provide insights, offer recommendations for managers and recommend future research directions.

Entrepreneurs could choose different corporate branding strategies from one extreme of "using one corporate name for all products" to another extreme of "using one brand name for each product". If entrepreneurs use one brand name for each product, they can build a clear image for each brand's target audience. However, the disadvantage is that the brand building investment is high, because consumers have resistance to brand switching when a new brand is introduced (Lam *et al.* 2010). The importance of the decision to pick a brand name for the company and for its products become more elevated since many new firms, if successful in their domestic markets, will consider entering the Chinese market. Chinese law requires every company to register a Chinese name before they start operating in China. Choosing a name for the China market is a big challenge because the Chinese language has thousands of characters, each with many meanings and with pronunciations that can vary from region to region (Fetscherin *et al.* 2012). See the P&G example in the box below.

P&G vs. Coca-Cola in China

P&G treats its corporate name and product brand names as separate and markets several products of a product category under one or more brand names. For P&G, the company name comes from the family names of its two founders (Procter and Gamble). P&G in English had no "suggestive" meaning for what is offered. When P&G had to register a company with a Chinese name in 1988 for its entry into the mainland China market, the leadership team in P&G Hong Kong asked a creative agency to propose a Chinese name for P&G. Eventually, 宝洁 (Chinese Pin-yin: Bao Jie) was chosen because the number one brand in terms of sales and profit for P&G Hong Kong in 1988 was Pampers, which has a Chinese name of 帮宝适 (Chinese Pin-yin: Bang Bao Shi, meaning: Help Baby Comfort). 宝洁 translates to 'baby clean' as 宝 (Bao) means "baby" and 洁 (Jie) means "clean". Later on, in the 1990s, P&G started offering many other brands/products in multiple categories. Unfortunately, the Chinese name was limiting because 'Baby Clean' was not congruent with P&G's wide variety of product categories.

When the Chinese name of P&G was decided by the Hong Kong team, they primarily thought about having the name with phonetic translation sounds similar to "Procter and Gamble", and did not consider creating a company name from a strategic point of view based on the future scope of business. For about two years in 1993–1994, P&G China top management forced all brand managers to limit their 30 seconds TV commercial duration to 28 seconds so that they could add a 2 second P&G corporate end-tag. The message was "P&G quality products make your life better". However, most creative agencies and brand managers resisted this change because managers of big P&G brands such as Rejoice, they did not want to spend a lot of media investment to build the corporate brand awareness of P&G. The awareness of the product brand, Rejoice, was much more important than the corporate brand of P&G to remind consumers to buy Rejoice. The managers of small brands or new brands in 1993–1994 also want to spend their limited marketing budget to build awareness of their brands, not building awareness of P&G's corporate brand P&G. In the end, the two-second end-tag requirement lasted only about two years. Although, we did not find any P&G spokesperson to publicly admit that the Chinese name of P&G was wrong, what we noticed was that P&G staff and other marketers simply referred P&G in English instead of Chinese. All Chinese with basic school education would have learned the 26 English letters of A–Z. So, P&G was easy for all Chinese to refer to anyway. The fact that Chinese referred to the English of P&G instead of its Chinese name indicated that the Chinese name for P&G was not as good as its Chinese name. Compare P&G's experience to Coca-Cola's. Coca-Cola, the first multinational firm allowed back in China in 1978, chose a very good Chinese name: 可口可乐 (Pin-yin: Ke Kou Ke Le), meaning "delicious happiness".

2. Brief Literature Review: Corporate Branding Strategies

The branding strategies of small- and medium-sized enterprises (SMEs) are somewhat different from large enterprises, So, we now discuss literature on SME branding strategies. SMEs had resource constraints in terms of time and money in hiring marketers for advertising and conducting marketing activities. As such, SMEs' approaches to the brand management style, operations, and functions are different from large enterprises. Prior studies found that trademarks registration and marketing expenses could create benefits in subsequent years and were likely to show a cumulative effect over time (Agostini *et al.* 2015). In addition, studies found that SMEs that focused on brands could achieve a distinct performance advantage over rivals by understanding customers' needs and brand perceptions, creating relevant and valued brands, supporting the brand consistently over time, effectively communicating the brand's identity to internal and external stakeholders and creating a coherent brand architecture (Berthon *et al.* 2008).

Some researchers studied drivers of brand credibility, defined as ability of the brand to deliver its promise, in consumer evaluation of global brands and domestic brands in an emerging market context (Srivastava *et al.* 2020). For global brands, perceived brand globalness and brand authenticity had a positive impact on brand credibility, but perceived local iconness had no significant influence because consumers may feel challenged to ascribe iconic associations as being a credible signal for global brands (Srivastava *et al.* 2020). For domestic brands, perceived brand globalness had a negative and significant effect on brand credibility. A possible reason for the negative effects of perceived brand globalness is that as domestic brands move into global markets to build brand value, emerging market consumers may feel that the domestic brand manifests a loss of commitment to its home market (Srivastava *et al.* 2020, p. 857).

More recently, prior studies noted the impact of the usage of the first- or second-person pronoun in the brand names, which was common in many products and companies such as iPhone or YouTube. Prior studies found that the usage of the first-person pronoun "I" and of the second-person pronoun "you" in a brand name could have positive impact on brand attitudes when they fit with the overall brand positioning (Kachersky and Carnevale 2015). The use of "you" had positive impact when the offering was positioned for its social benefits, while the use of "I", had greater positive impact when the offering was positioned for its personal benefits (Kachersky and Carnevale 2015).

The marketing investment of building two different names (a company name and a product brand name) is higher than that of building only one name. However, there are major long-term implications for marketing and for the business development of a company. The cost saving of using one name for two purposes, corporate brand image and product brand image, could limit the long-term growth of a company.

When companies grow from small companies into big multinational companies, these companies might have the same name as the product brand name and the company name. As marketing budgets were limited when the company was small, marketers tended to put all the money for different activities into building one name that benefited both the product brand and company brand.

3. Lessons Learned from GoGoVan and LaLaMove

Should company use the name "van" or "move"? The case of GoGoVan and LaLaMove can be an excellent example. Both GoGoVan and LaLaMove provided a platform to connect drivers with people who had to deliver goods. Both companies were founded in 2013 in Hong Kong and branched out of Hong Kong into Southeast Asia and China. Both companies attracted prominent investors from Mainland China and other countries after these expansions (Leung 2017). GoGoVan was Hong Kong's first unicorn with a valuation of over $1 billion in September 2017 following a merger deal with the China-based 58 Suyun (Russell 2017). 58 Suyun was the freight division of 58 Home, a subsidiary of the New York-listed 58.com. 58 Home owned the majority of the merged entity after the merger and brought together backers such as Tencent and Alibaba. The merger would also create Asia's largest online platform in the intracity logistics and freight business (Perez 2017). The first step for the combined entity was to run GoGoVan services in the 40 cities where 58 Suyun operated and expand the combined coverage to 100 cities in the following 12 months (Barreto and Zhu 2017). In October 2017, LaLaMove received a valuation that was just below $1 billion mark (Russell 2017) after announcing its Series C funding of $100 million led by mainland's VC firm, ShunWei Capital, which was cofounded by Xiaomi's chief executive Lei Jun (Leung 2017).

Both GoGoVan and LaLaMove offered transportation and logistics services on-demand, very much in the same style that Uber works for passengers (Russell 2017). They were the Uber models of urban transportation for moving things, not people (Horwitz 2014). LaLaMove founder and CEO Shing Chow (Chow) estimated the logistics market in China alone was worth $1.7 trillion a year, and Uber was among those to take a look at the possibilities (Russell 2017). Uber had tried a logistic model in Hong Kong, but its "Uber Cargo" service was eliminated less than two years after its launch (Russell 2017). Although Uber could not do it on its own with enough income to sustain, it did not give up. Uber identified partner for synergy and income. On July 19, 2018, Uber had a press release to announce its exclusive global partnership with Cargo, the startup that provided in-car commerce to the rideshare economy. The partnership aimed to delight riders with snacks, beverages, electronics, and beauty products while on a trip (Uber and Cargo 2018). As of November 2020, Uber and Cargo had teamed up to increase rideshare earnings with Uber's cartop display program.[1]

In fact, Both GoGoVan and LaLaMove were similar in company names when they were founded in 2013. Both had "Van" in their company names, "GoGoVan" and "EasyVan". In 2014, EasyVan decided to rebrand as LaLaMove just in time for its launch in Bangkok because it would offer services from vehicles, such as motorcycles, that were not vans (Horwitz 2014). In an interview by Apple Daily, a Chinese newspaper in Hong Kong, Chow, Lalamove's founder, said that when EasyVan was founded, its main competitor was GoGoVan (*Apple Daily News* 2017). However, as GoGoVan exploited its first mover advantage, EasyVan decided to enter the South East Asia Market in 2014 and realized that motorcycles were more popular than vans in Bangkok. Bangkok was not the only country for such change in company name from EasyVan to LaLaMove. The other countries also had different transportation vehicles which were not vans. Therefore, Chow changed the company name to LaLaMove and added services from motorcycles.

---

[1]The cartop display program allows driver to install a display on top of his vehicle to show ads while he drives to make extra cash (Drivecargo.com 2020).

The Chinese name for GoGoVan was 高高客货车(Kim 2014) with Pin-yin of "Gao Gao Ke Huo Che". Gao meant "high" in English and has a sound similar to "Go" in English. The three Chinese characters of "Ke Huo Che" is the Chinese phrase for van, while "Ke" means "customer", "Huo" means "goods" and "Che" means "car". About one year ago, GoGoVan changed its company name to GoGoX. So, the founders also realized the limitation of using Van only for its platform.

The Chinese name for LaLaMove is 货拉拉 and has a Pin-yin of "Huo La La". "Huo" means "goods" and "La" means "move". Therefore, the decision of Chow to change the name of EasyVan to LaLaMove was consistent with the proposal to use benefit/job to be done for consumers in the company name, "move goods". If Lalamove is a corporate name, it can have product name such as EasyVan under it (Lalamove EasyVan) for matching the two sides of the platform: those who need Van and those who drive Van. Similarly, it can have Lalamove EasyBike for matching the two sides of the platform: those who need bicycles and those who ride bicycles.

4. Insights, Recommendations and Research Results

In this section, we identify and offer insights, recommendations and research results pertinent to the question of what company names are currently being suggested and what they should suggest. Entrepreneurs have several approaches to create suggestive company names. First, they use names such as Burger King, Pizza Hut, Kentucky Fried Chicken (KFC) to suggest "corporate ability in a product category" for different types of food categories. Second, simply use names of founders to create company names. Examples include Li Ning from China and McDonald's from the US. Third, create special suggestive company name. Examples include Alibaba and Baidu from China, Amazon and Google from the US. Baidu is the Chinese pin-yin for 百度. Bai means hundred. Du means angle. So, the two Chinese characters together mean hundred angles or directions. These two Chinese characters are also included in a Chinese poem. It describes how a man searches a lady from hundred directions. Fourth, the mission and purpose of the company expressed as the benefit that company can bring to consumers. Example is LaLaMove as mentioned earlier.

For Google, for example, the term "google" itself is a creative spelling of googol, a number equal to 10 to the 100th power (Dictionary.com 2020). The Chinese name for Google has two Chinese characters 谷歌 (Pin-yin: Gu Ge) which is a phonetic translation for Google. The English back translation for the first Chinese character 谷 is "valley" and for the second Chinese character 歌 is "song". So, Chinese will not get the original meaning of Google from the Chinese name.

The case of GoGoVan and LaLaMove showed the importance of getting the name right when a company was formed. It was also important to know whether using a suggestive company name of "van" was better or worse than the other naming alternative of using "move". Therefore, we followed Zhang and Schmitt (2001) and Lam *et al.* (2013) and used a concept test to quantitatively measure consumers' reaction to four different overall concepts created from two company concepts with two company names (GoGoVan or LaLaMove) using an experimental approach as follows.

We emphasized the Chinese company name in larger and bold typeface in the experimental instrument, that is, the concept board shown to respondents. For the two company concepts, we created a "van" concept using the App description for the GoGoVan App and created a "move" concept using the App description for the LaLaMove App. These descriptions would be shown to any individual before he/she decided to download the App. People who had installed these apps were excluded from the study. As a result, we had a total of four concepts. First, the "van" company concept with the "GoGoVan" company name. Second, the "van" company concept with the "LaLaMove" company name. Third, the "move" company concept with the "LaLaMove" company name. Fourth, the "move" company concept with the "GoGoVan" company name.

A research agency conducted the research fieldwork in a central location in Beijing in January 2019. The researchers conducted 400 interviews among adults (age over 18), and randomly assigned them to one of the four concepts (50% male and 50% female, with an average age of 34). For the company name, we used the four measures, liking, memorability, impact of image, and name's fit with concept, to capture participants' responses toward the company name. We used a 7-point scale for all metrics. We conducted statistical significance tests at the 95% confidence level, and we showed the research results in Table 1. The five key findings were summarized as follows for the results of on company concepts and company names.

First, we compare row "b" with row "a" in Table 1. For the company concept of "van", the use of LaLaMove as a company name could generate significantly higher overall liking, purchase intention, credibility, uniqueness, relevancy scores on the company concept than the use of GoGoVan as a company name. Furthermore, "LaLaMove" as a company name could also generate significantly higher overall liking, memorability, impact on image and name's fit with concept.

Second, we compare row "c" with row "d" in Table 1. For the company concept of "move", the use of LaLaMove as a company name also generated significantly higher overall liking, purchase intention, credibility, uniqueness, and relevancy scores than the use of GoGoVan as a company name. "LaLaMove" as a company name could also generate significantly higher overall liking, memorability, impact on image and name's fit with concept.

Third, if we use the same company name, "GoGoVan", then using "move" as a company concept was better than using "van" as a company concept for generating significantly higher overall liking, purchase intention and credibility (by comparing row "d" with row "a" in Table 1). If we use the same company name, "LaLaMove", then using "move" as a company concept also was better than using "van" as a company concept for generating significantly higher overall liking, purchase intention, credibility, uniqueness and relevancy (by comparing column "c" with column "b" in Table 1).

Fourth, we could compare row "c" with row "a" in Table 1. The use of the "move" company concept with the "LaLaMove" company name generated significantly higher overall liking, purchase intention, credibility, uniqueness, and relevancy scores than the use of the "van" company concept with the "GoGoVan" company name. The "LaLaMove" name was also significantly better than "GoGoVan" in this comparison because of the significantly higher scores on overall liking, memorability, impact on image and name's fit with concept.

Table 1. Research results.

Combination Company concept + Company name	#	Overall Liking Mean (95% CI)		Purchase Intention Mean (95% CI)		Company Concept Credibility Mean (95% CI)		Uniqueness Mean (95% CI)		Relevancy Mean (95% CI)	
GoGoVan GoGoVan	a	4.7	(4.5–4.9)	4.53	(4.35–4.71)	4.37	(4.18–4.56)	4.08	(3.87–4.29)	4.18	(4–4.36)
GoGoVan LaLaMove	b	5.25	(5.07–5.43)	5.51	(5.36–5.66)	4.98	(4.82–5.14)	4.59	(4.38–4.8)	5.16	(4.94–5.38)
LaLaMove LaLaMove	c	5.71	(5.57–5.85)	5.88	(5.73–6.03)	5.49	(5.31–5.67)	4.95	(4.77–5.13)	5.43	(5.21–5.65)
LaLaMove GoGoVan	d	5.11	(4.92–5.30)	4.87	(4.69–5.05)	4.89	(4.68–5.10)	4.55	(4.34–4.76)	4.66	(4.43–4.89)
Multiple Comparisons		$c > b, d, a$; b and $d > a$;		$c > b > d > a$		$c > a, b, d$; b and $d > a$		$c > a, d$; b and $d > a$		c and $b > d > a$	

Company Name

Combination Company concept + Company name	#	Overall Liking Mean (95% CI)		Memorability Mean (95% CI)		Impact on Image Mean (95% CI)		Name's Fit with Concept Mean (95% CI)	
GoGoVan GoGoVan	a	4.01	(3.76–4.26)	3.61	(3.33–3.89)	4.33	(4.16–4.5)	4.28	(4.09–4.47)
GoGoVan LaLaMove	b	5.53	(5.37–5.69)	5.77	(5.58–5.96)	5.39	(5.25–5.53)	5.39	(5.24–5.54)
LaLaMove LaLaMove	c	5.68	(5.5–5.86)	5.97	(5.79–6.15)	5.64	(5.49–5.79)	5.71	(5.54–5.88)
LaLaMove GoGoVan	d	4.32	(4.07–4.57)	3.73	(3.45–4.01)	4.51	(4.31–4.71)	4.69	(4.48–4.90)
Multiple Comparisons		c and $b > d > a$		c and $b > d > a$		c and $b > d > a$		c and $b > d > a$	

Note: We used the Post Hoc Tests for Multiple Comparisons and only the statistically significant mean difference ($p < 0.05$) among a, b, c, d were shown.

5. Conclusions, Limitations and Future Research Directions

We proposed and empirically demonstrated that if a company name was suggestive of the key business of the corporation and the consumer needs it satisfies, it generates significantly higher scores when measuring a company's concept and when measuring a company's name. Because the actual name used is so important, marketers should take the naming task seriously and ask creative agencies to propose names using the proposals and research findings in this chapter.

Chapter Takeaways

- Use a suggestive name and to use the same name for both the new product and for the new company; the selected name should suggest the job that the product and company could perform for the company's customer.
- Naming is strategic and should be considered from a long-term perspective, as the focus is not solely on the success of launching one single product but also on creating a successful company.
- If entrepreneurs want to incorporate a new company to do business in China, they are required by the government to have a Chinese company name. Although an English company name is not required, it is better to have both Chinese and English company names when the company is formed. Then, there won't be a need to go through company name registration/name addition process to add an English company name.

Our research has a few limitations. We had only studied startup companies in transportation, namely, GoGoVan and LaLaMove. We hope this chapter will encourage more researchers to test suggestive company names in other industries and report their findings. We expect that results will be similar in other fast moving consumer goods (FMCG) industries. For more expensive products (e.g., refrigerators, washing machines) with longer purchase cycle, buyers will likely choose a company/product after going through rational comparison of the key attributes of different products. The effect of the name of a company or product may be less significant than the case for FMCG industries.

In terms of cultures and countries, we conducted the fieldwork for this study in Beijing and the questionnaire was in Chinese. Because different languages require a different number of characters to express the same meaning, the total number of characters and pronunciations required to express a name may be longer in English than in Chinese. The total number of characters and pronunciations might affect a respondents' comprehension of different names as a whole. In the Chinese education system, students study Chinese language before they get admission into university. They have to learn many Chinese phases with four Chinese characters, and also use these phases in their daily conversations and in major festivals too. For example, in the Chinese New Year, they will wish their friends 身体健康 (Pin-yin: Shen Ti Jian Kang) which means "healthy body". As a result, marketer could use different combinations of four Chinese characters to create memorable and likeable taglines for their brands when entering the Chinese market. A watch brand, Titus, had used a total of 14 Chinese characters in its selling line as follows:

不在乎天长地久 (Pin-yin: Bu Zai Hu Tian Zhang De Jiu)
只在乎曾经拥有 (Pin-yin: Zhi Zai Hu Ceng Jing Yong You)

For Chinese, the first three Chinese characters in the first line (Bu Zai Hu) and the first three Chinese characters in the second line (Zhi Zai Hu) have contrast. The second and the third characters are the same (Zai Hu) which means "care" in English. The first character in the first line, "Bu", means "no". The first character in the second line, "Zhi", means "only". So, together, the sentence structure for the first line and the second line means "I don't care" and "I only care". The remaining four Chinese characters in the first line "Tian Zhang De Jiu" and in the second line "Ceng Jing Yong You" are popular Chinese phases with four Chinese characters and so Chinese can easily understand their meaning. "Tian Zhang De Jiu" means "as long as heaven and earth". "Ceng Jing Yong You" means "as short as a moment of us together".

So, the meaning in English for these 14 Chinese characters is:

I don't care how long heaven and earth will last.
I only care about the short moment of us together.

References

Agostini, L., Nosella, A., and Filippini, R. (2015). Brand — Building efforts and their association with SME sales performance, *Journal of Small Business Management*, 53, 161–173. 10.1111/jsbm.12185.

Apple Daily News (2017). EasyVan 改名 Lalamove, Call 車貨運平台攻電單車突圍 (English back translation from author — EasyVan changed name to LaLaMove. Platform for calling vehicles for delivery offered motorcycles as well to achieve breakthrough). https://hk.finance.appledaily.com/finance/daily/article/20170620/20061974 (accessed on January 20, 2019).

Barreto, E. and Zhu, J. (2017). HK's GOGOVAN, China's 58 Suyun follow merger with $200 mln fundraising, Market News, *Reuters*, August 31, 2017. https://www.reuters.com/article/hongkong-gogovan-fundraising/hks-gogovan-chinas-58-suyun-follow-merger-with-200-mln-fundraising-idUSL4N1LH3N5 (accessed on January 20, 2019).

Berthon, P., Ewing, M. T., and Napoli, J. (2008). Brand management in small to medium-sized enterprises, *Journal of Small Business Management*, 46(1), 27–45.

Dictionary.com (2020). November 5, 2020. https://www.dictionary.com/browse/google.

Drivecargo.com (2020). November 7, 2020. https://drivecargo.com.

Fetscherin, M., Alon, I., Littrell, R., and Chan, A. (2012). In China? Pick your brand name carefully, *Harvard Business Review*, 90(9), 26.

Horwitz, J. (2014). Hong Kong's Easyvan rebrands as Lalamove just in time for launch in Bangkok, *TechinAsia*, November 27, 2014. https://www.techinasia.com/hong-kongs-easyvan-rebrands-as-lalamove-just-in-time-for-launch-in-bangkok (accessed on January 20, 2019).

Kachersky, L. and Carnevale, M. (2015). Effects of pronoun brand name perspective and positioning on brand attitude, *Journal of Product and Brand Management*, 24(2), 157–164.

Kim, Y.-H. (2014). 人人投资的高高客货车要解决大城市物流难题 (English back translation from author: RenRen invested in GoGoVan to solve the logistic difficulty in big cities), *The Wall Street Journal (simplified Chinese edition)*. https://cn.wsj.com/articles/CN-TEC-20141118173807 (accessed on January 20, 2019).

Lam, P. Y., Chan, A., Gopaoco, H., Oh, K., and So, T. H. (2013). Dual branding strategy for a successful new product launch in China, *Business Horizons*, 56(5), 583–589.

Lam, S. K., Ahearne, M., Hu, Ye., and Schillewaert, N. Resistance to brand switching when a radically new brand is introduced: A social identity theory perspective, *Journal of Marketing*, 74(6), pp. 128–146.

Leung, H. (2017). Lalamove scores $100M investment from China: Is this Hong Kong's next unicorn? *Forbes*, October 10, 2017. https://www.forbes.com/sites/hannahleung/2017/10/10/lalamove-scores-100m-investment-from-china-is-this-hong-kongs-next-unicorn/#242c164136a3. (accessed on April 1, 2021).

Perez, B. (2017). GoGoVan to become Hong Kong's first US$1 billion start-up after merger with 58 Suyun, *South China Morning Post*. August 28, 2017. https://www.scmp.com/tech/china-tech/article/2108658/gogovan-become-hong-kongs-first-us1-billion-start-after-merger-58.

Russell, J. (2017). Logistics on-demand startup Lalamove raises $100M as it approaches a $1B valuation. *Techcrunch*, October 10, 2017. https://techcrunch.com/2017/10/10/lalamove-raises-100m/ (accessed on January 20, 2019).

Srivastava, A., Dey, D. K., and Balaji, M. S. (2020). Drivers of brand credibility in consumer evaluation of global brands and domestic brands in an emerging market context, *Journal of Product and Brand Management*, 29(7), pp. 849–861. https://doi.org/10.1108/JPBM-03-2018-1782.

Uber and Cargo (2018). November 7, 2020. https://drivecargo.com/en-us/uber.

Zhang, S. and Schmitt, B. H. (2001). Creating local brands in multilingual international markets, *Journal of Marketing Research*, 38(3), 313–325.

Using Neuro-Linguistic Programming to Build the Foundation of Brands: A Guide for Chinese Firms

Rodney A. Josephson

1. Introduction

When entering foreign markets, the challenges of transposing intercultural ideas across vastly different cultures pose great obstacles because the intended brand image may be misperceived, possibly damaging the firm. For example, Fuke Foods (Shishi) Ltd., from Quanzhou, Fujian in China has a product called "儿童营养肉松", which can be translated as "Shredded Meat Product, for Children". When entering Western markets, the company wanted to translate and use an English product name, and unfortunately incorrectly described their product as "Child Shredded Meat" (Figure 1). To minimize such branding mishaps when entering foreign markets, this chapter provides a handbook using neuro-linguistic programming (NLP), which would especially be useful for Chinese small- and medium-sized enterprises (SMEs).

Figure 1. "Child Shredded Meat" by Fuke Foods.

Humankind can learn or acquire language and communicate a general perception, believing that it is sufficient to use in complex business matters, especially marketing and branding-related activities. However, there are deep complexities to understanding language and culture. Even in a large-scale, top-ranked business, employees may not know the full meaning of the communication characteristics used within that particular sector. This chapter is based on the premise that there are hidden elements to communication that can be understood and tapped for more significant adaptation of a brand's image in the mind's synaptic network or memory.

Many SMEs may lack various capabilities and access to resources to effectively apply integrated marketing communications when entering foreign markets. Since integrated marketing communications brings all types of messages together, connecting the processes as a whole in managing a brand's image, maintaining the original meaning is crucial. How the firm maintains its company values, image, and quality while also transposing its ideas to create and build a brand internationally requires identity management through all the media channels in every market it operates poses significant challenges. To do so, firms need to have a better understanding of memory formation and the true meaning of words and symbols in different markets. By employing NLP tools, Chinese SMEs may have the possibility of greater success in achieving their goals in foreign markets.

The first step in doing so is mastering the English language (Chiang 2009). Zhang *et al.* (2013, p. 18) state that English, being a borrower, is now based on tens of other languages, mainly Latin and French, and possesses the largest vocabulary of all languages: more than a million words. Therefore, learning English is a daunting task, especially the source meanings of the words.

A Tidbit of Wisdom
"When you master your mind, you master your world".
Language and images program the mind, thus to control the language input, one controls the output and behavior.

---

2. Brand Image — How an Impression Forms in the Mind

Laws and regulations influence the branding of goods and services. For instance, larger corporations generally have full-time lawyers checking compliance, initiating trademark infringement suits against potential threats. An example is *Red Bull vs. Andale Energy Drink LLC*, where Red Bull GmbH accused Andale Energy Drink Co., LLC of multiple complaints regarding the graphical representation "mark" of their trademark allegedly too close to their brand stating "false suggestion of a connection Trademark Act Section 2(a) Priority and likelihood of confusion in the design", thus filing the infringement case.[1] Further, it is alleged "both depict (and would be recognized as) rectangular flags" and "asserts a *bona fide* intent-to-use Applicant's Opposed Marks are identical or very similar to, used for the same or similar purposes, and/or are or will be advertised and promoted to and directed at the same trade channels, the same purchasers, and are or will be used in the same environment as Opposer Red Bull's products and related goods and services". Finally "is likely to cause confusion, mistake or deception among purchasers, users, and the public, thereby damaging Red Bull". Therefore, it is crucial to know the processes, methods, and linguistics in-depth in brand creation since the Chinese SMEs attempting to enter a new market may be challenged by a major player, or anyone for that matter, with plenty of resources to keep their market share.

---

[1] *Red Bull GmbH v. Jean Pierre Biane Red Bull GmbH v. Andale Energy Drink Co.*, LLC. https://ttabcenter.com/ttabcase/red-bull-gmbh-v-jean-pierre-biane-red-bull-gmbh-v-andale-energy-drink-co-llc-2/ (accessed on January 21, 2021).

The image of Andale! was considered to be confusing and an infringement of Red Bull's trademark.

Brand image is a key component of the brand's equity as it conveys value to consumers. Image is defined as "the set of beliefs, ideas, and impressions that a person holds regarding an object" (Kotler 2001, p. 273). Correspondingly, the brand image refers to the mental representation the individual shapes based on beliefs, ideas, and impressions of the brand. The social semiotic approach to building corporate identity and brand equity should address their morphology and symbolic meanings for that target market in question (Chiang 2009; Schmitt 1994). However, what if we can transpose, develop, and create that brand image in the receiver's mind via NLP in intercultural communications? Bandler and Grinder (1975, pp. 7–9) propose the following regarding how the human brain and nervous system work and perceive reality:

> there is an irreducible difference between the world and our experience of it. We, as human beings, do not operate directly on the world. Each of us creates a representation of the world in which we live … The suggestion is that the function of the brain and nervous system, and sense organs are in the main eliminative and not productive. Each person is at each moment capable of remembering all that has ever happened to him … The function of the brain and the nervous system is to protect us from being

overwhelmed and confused by this mass of largely useless and irrelevant knowledge by shutting out most of what we should otherwise perceive or remember at any moment and leaving only that very small and special selection which is likely to be practically useful.

Communication is defined as a transactional process between two or more parties, where meaning is exchanged via intentional use of symbols such as words, pictures, music, and other sensory stimulants for conveying thoughts (Blythe 2000). Communication of any kind can influence the receiver's perception of reality, even if the messages are factual or fantasy. There are various methods through which the impression is formed in memory, such as via social media, TV, books, radio, face-to-face, and the like. The consumer will perceive the message differently based on the methods and language used to convey the brand image being employed, creating new views or misrepresentations of the presented information (Bandler and Grinder 1975). The consumer experiences the messages differently also due to the five different human senses (O'Connor and Seymour 1994). Consider the difference between TV commercials and magazine ads: a TV commercial uses actors adding drama to the material, product placements, and celebrity endorsements or associations to the brand, while in the written ad, there are fewer methods to stimulate and persuade the reader unless they are more directly stated — only our reading ability and imagination are used. These channels have vastly different effects on the audience, so the marketer needs to grasp those critical points based on the neuroscience of linguistics and communication since one channel may attract and another sensory channel may deter the buyer.

Once the impression is formed in the mind, it is difficult to change, especially when recorded in long-term memory (Walvis 2008), within a specific culture and environment, and via repetition and other sensory stimuli (Skinner *et al.* 2003). For example, many Chinese perceive "foreign brands as global brands from the imagined West" (Tian and Dong 2011, p. 6). Note the word "imagined" is essential because we perceive something based on what we have learned from media or education, which goes for all countries and cultures. Thus, the marketing of any good or service would be subjected to the same phenomenon as stated prior, and therefore, it is of great importance to understanding the power of different media forms using a neuro-linguistic approach.

There is also the issue of Chinese and English being different linguistic systems. "The Chinese language adopts a logographic writing system in the form of sign symbols or characters, while the English language uses a phonographic writing system in the form of alphabet or letters" (Chiang 2009, pp. 333–334).

We begin the process to create that perception based on the definition of NLP:

> Neuro-Linguistic Programming, a name that encompasses the three most influential components of producing human experience: neurology, language, and programming. The neurological system regulates how our bodies function, language determines how we interface and communicate with other people, and our programming determines the kinds of models of the world we create. Neuro-Linguistic Programming describes the fundamental dynamics between mind (neuro) and language (linguistic) and how their interplay affects our body and behavior (programming).[2] (Dilts 1999)

Next, we will cover some general concepts and theories, language structures with situations and examples of how they work and what they imply, the meaning of words, and how to deal with some of the possibilities we face in business; and how to possibly handle and manage the marketing plan so that you may consider alternative strategies of building a solid corporate identity and brand equity.

A well-crafted brand image should create a tangible concept that will reverberate in the receiver's mind, regardless of whether the receiver wants or needs the good or service as it is fixed in long-term memory (Tian and Dong 2011). We can consider the initial branding of an idea as the Seven Seconds rule (Coffee and Phillips 2010) — the receiver will store the first impression of the brand in its overall form deep in the memory, and thus the consumer makes decisions based on their memory of it (Walvis 2008). For example, a song is one way we remember from

---

[2]Dilts, R. B. (1999). NLP Definition. http://www.nlpu.com/NLPU_WhatIsNLP.html (accessed October 25, 2020).

TV commercials or learning the English alphabet in which the message is placed in our long-term memory from repetitive processes. Consequently, the goal of a well-crafted marketing plan would be to create a compelling brand image summarized in three main points: memorability, positive image, and legality (Cui 2019).

The personality of the brand should consist of multi-sensational (i.e., see, feel, hear, taste, and even smell), which would build on the following (Sheena 2012): "Consumers' ability to recall a brand name is regarded as 'one of the best predictors' of a brand's success" (Gontijo and Zhang 2007, p. 32). What we are referring to is the contextual *emotional response* of associating the brand to connect with the consumer's past emotions and or memories to secure it in the consumers' neuro-pathways thoroughly and their biological system, that is, "the emotional underpinning of a brand" (Gordon 2002, p. 119). Emotions play a key role in communication and learning styles (Walvis 2008). We will discuss methods of contextually connecting feelings and emotions via language later on in this chapter. To summarize, we could contend that the created brand image should be planted in the consumer's mind to continually excite the synaptic vesicles and expand in the neuro-pathways and managed by mastering the tools of NLP.

There are many factors involved in memory function, including a range of filters such as social and cultural conditions that affect each person's own experiences and memories, in which human beings may use to distort, generalize, and delete what is received in any form of information from the external world (Bandler and Grinder 1975). It would also include each person's internally represented experiences in their given sensory modalities of preference.

Studies show that each person processes every interaction in the external environment, which is called "system representations" in NLP: pictures, sounds, feelings, language, etc. Those studies show that people tend to have preferences for their chosen modalities or sensory representation systems in which each interaction is coded (O'Connor and McDermott 1996). Human beings create and build their representations of the world they live in through internal coding by their sensory representational systems (Bandler and Grinder 1975). A visual person will generally code their experiences based on pictures "in their mind's eye", feelings will generally be coded as the term kinaesthetic, and an auditory person will tend to code with sounds they hear (Brown and Turnbull 2000). Taste and smell are usually included in a person's kinaesthetic system, which is part of the three central systems used to represent the world internally. Therefore, marketers should consider these modalities' relevance in branding.

Human beings have the ability to imagine, have memories that can associate ideas and concepts that affect their understanding and approach to consuming or purchasing a product. Let me illustrate this for an insurance policy. Using the example of having bought car insurance from an agent of "X" (X means the company or brand) offering policy "Y". If an accident happened "Z", the agent of "X" would serve some of the benefits of that policy "Y" to cover "Z". So, the agent is the physical element serving the potential "Y" to solve "Z".

If a person buys "X" as a whole annual service package from that particular agent, it is a complete concept formed in the consumer's mind as a so-called thing or object (a package), we could consider this package imaginary — like a cartoon. The potential buyer has probably been bombarded with 100s of advertisements explaining how it works, who is involved, and what those policies will cover. Thus, the pure service policies and benefits have been shaped in consumers' minds by advertisements, governed by laws and contracts, making it a *tangible* and *stored* service. As a visual interpretation below, we can see that the *brand image creator* manifests the perceived concept into a physical, 3D type object through artwork, linguistics, media channels, or even physical elements that represent what is to be sold to the buyer. The *consumer* perceives and experiences neuro-physiological influences of the *brand image* from various media channels where they will interact with an *agent or representative.*

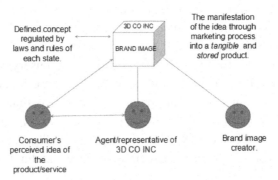

How Chinese or other foreign SMEs connect to their customers is crucial for their success, and the following is but one method in a motto for creating a *pure service*: "You're In Good Hands With Allstate®", which is the motto the insurance company uses in its advertising. The company explains how this motto was created:

> Ellis, general sales manager, creates the "You're In Good Hands With Allstate®" slogan in 1950 to demonstrate our commitment to our customers. It is inspired by his daughter's recent hospitalization, during which Ellis' wife was reassured that, under the doctor's care, her daughter "was in good hands".

This motto supports the notion that marketing creates an idea that becomes an object or living concept, that is a [brand] in the receiver's mind using the sensory language of feeling and caring, of which "The theory of self-consistency emphasizes the resonance and the emotional transfer between consumers and brands" is suggested by Li and Zhao (2018, pp. 237–248).

Insurance could be considered as an objective, physical thing in the mind's eye of the consumer due to the suggestions or pre-programming from at least three methods by which advertising can shape the consumers' perceptions of product quality: (1) by providing information about product attributes (modalitites in NLP), (learning theory: Hovland *et al.* 1953; Lavidge and Steiner 1961; McGuire 1978), (2) by increasing the target buyer's familiarity with the brand (mere exposure theory: Wilson 1979; Zajonc 1980; Sawyer 1981), and (3) by shaping and modifying the consumer's attitude toward the ad (attitude-toward-the-ad-theory: Mitchell and Olson 1981; MacKenzie *et al.* 1986; Brown and Stayman 1992). It has been proposed that it happens in a law-like regularity that justifies three branding laws that contribute to the integration of neuro-biology within the field of brand management (Walvis 2008).

Another type of service experience is restaurants. A world leader in the fast foods sector, KFC, has been using the following motto in its branding: "Finger Lickin' Good". Notice the sensory words of *feel* and *taste* in the message being sent to the consumer even if they have never had that food before. However, can that motto's socio-linguistic message be transposed properly, and will it be suitable to use in the idea of licking fingers in different cultures? "Lickin'" is a shortening of *licking*, while the motto's idea may be considered a *metaphor* and may only be suitable inside English-speaking countries. For example, Chinese consumers generally use plastic gloves when eating such foods; thus, "*Finger Lickin'*" may not be transferable or beneficial to use in the Chinese context.

Courtesy of S. Durmusoglu

Another point is that in English, making up words as syllables may not correspond to the morphemes, unlike in Chinese, where meaning and sound are connected. What this means is that in the Chinese system of writing, words are mainly formed combining meaningful units as opposed to meaningless sounds. Chinese is a logographic writing system and is generally more transparent than English since it is based on graphemes, which are most meaningful, whereas in English the syllables may not correspond to the morphemes and thus a meaningless word could be created (Basciano 2016).

> … In Chinese you cannot dissociate meaning from sound: whereas in a language like English, where syllables do not necessarily correspond to morphemes, one can make up a word without any meaning, in a Chinese made-up word like, say, 肺哄 fèi-hǒng, each component has a meaning of its own, respectively 'lung' and 'fool, coax', despite the fact that the word we created as a whole does not make any sense. These

differences deeply affect the process of brand naming: in European languages such as English, brand names mostly rely on sound appeal (e.g., Cohen 1995), while in Chinese semantics plays a key role, and the meaning of the constituents in a name must be chosen wisely. (Basciano 2016, p. 250)

Therefore, if the Chinese firm used this approach to branding messages in the western market, it might not be culturally or linguistically acceptable.

3. NLP — The Neuroscience of Marketing

In the previous sections, we covered the general concept of neurolinguistics; this part will cover NLP or the *neurological branding maxim*, delving deep into the human senses such as visual, kinaesthetic, auditory, olfactory, and gustatory channels of human communication within one's environment. The goal is to understand that there are multiple communication parts to analyze and comprehend based on linguistics. By knowing those elements, we can formalize a brand image where the etymological aspects of language combined with psychological factors will result in a solid, well-formed, and contextually appropriate brand image. Words and sentence structures have various deep complexities in their different print meanings than auditory, as just one example. While we may create a new word that may be meaningless, there could be associations to that creation that may cause various effects on the receiver, be it only a word or graphical combination of the two.

"Homophony is when a set of words are pronounced identically, but have different meanings. It is not necessary for homophonic words to be spelled the same way, which is called homography" (Basciano 2016, p. 251). For instance, the homophonic sounds of words are generally fixed, but the spelling is different in the following examples: *clause* (sentence structure), *claws* (long nails), *Claus* (name). In Chinese, "马路 *mǎlù* 'road', 马鹿 *mǎlù* 'red deer,' 马陆 *mǎlù* 'millipede'" (Basciano 2016, p. 251). When we hear one of these words, we would not know what they refer to unless there is context to that particular word. Nevertheless, we should consider that regardless of the context, the brain should process all three words if we are told any one of them in a discussion. We could contend if one said [claws] in a contextually appropriate sentence, the mind would potentially see all possible meanings (Claus, clause, claws) to that homophonic sound and choose the appropriate one to fit the context. It should be important to know all of the possible meanings associated with a given word to determine whether it is appropriate to use in the market in question. There could be a branding strategy to use words with multiple meanings to attract the consumer that we will discuss later in the chapter.

NLP is a tool to understand the deeper sensory meanings of communication parts to formalize a brand image's foundation from a multidimensional perspective so that you can build an intrigue or mysterious sense to the intended concept. We can also add numerology to the foundation of NLP, among others, to better grasp the elements of communication strategies.

Other areas to consider are communication styles within each culture, matching and mismatching of language patterns in the culture, brand image rapport within the culture, and a host of other crucial psychological and physiological challenges adding to a successful brand image. We need to consider the different media channels available, such as social media, video-based, print, or even face-to-face. There are various techniques to instill the brand in one's mind by creating strong links within the brain's synaptic network. Walvis (2008, p.186) continues regarding his three propositions:

> In sum, the three theses provide a neurological branding maxim: create as many synaptic connections as possible (richness) between the neural representations of primary choice cues and the brand name (relevance), and reactivate these connections regularly through a specific message (coherence).

The key is to build as many synaptic connections to the brand image or personality, and that is where mastering the concept of NLP and related fields come into play. The goal is to make a coherent brand image using the most stimulating colors, shapes, words, and branding methods applicable to that particular business model and target buyer's context. The methodologies and tools of NLP may be the best approach to master for creating a successful brand image.

We should consider cross-cultural differences since each society perceives what a brand personality is within that defined context, and thus what one culture deems as appropriate may reject (Cui 2019). For instance, the average Chinese consumer may enjoy more relaxed settings, nature-oriented concepts such as flowers, sleeping pandas, luck, etc., while the American counterpart may be more aggressive, shooting guns and watching kickboxing matches (Schmitt 1994). Therefore, we could conclude that using one's own cultural and linguistic approach to build a brand and enter a new market may have negative results as they are disassociated from the behavioral and linguistic connections.

4. A Deeper, Hidden Meaning — The Governing Codes and Structures of Language and Media

A Tidbit of Wisdom
"The foundation of the house builds the true home".
It is the root and foundation of something that governs all.

"Ye who builds or knows the foundation is the master of the house", we could say. The marketer should master the foundation of communication — the deep code if you will. How the consumer perceives the aesthetic quality of the sign or message intended to brand the identity of the company's name and motto, goods and services consist of symbolism from different cultures, languages and structures, characters, categorization of information, and value structures (Schmidt 1994). Those elements should be of great importance in knowing the foundations for building a successful brand within Western or other markets.

In human language, a word is created to serve a purpose, of which the foundation of a word is called its *etymology*. Over time, the [base] words may gain multiple associations, including phonetic meanings, which in metaphorical terms would mean: *adding paint to walls to cover up the old layer*, but the house's foundation will always stand; otherwise, the house will collapse. We should note that most languages have come from other languages or have been influenced by them, especially the English language, thus complicating the matter to communicate across cultures. However, the original word of that source language is still the same governing code — numerology.

It would be of great benefit that the marketer knows the historical foundations of a language and culture to create a successful brand image and minimize cross-cultural misunderstandings. Basciano (2016, p. 251) gives an example of a major Chinese firm attempting entry into the US market:

> The leading Chinese soft drink company 健力宝 jiàn lì-bǎo "healthy-power-treasure", very successful in China and Southeast Asia was not welcomed in the USA, where the company chose to use the pinyin transcription Jianlibao. The product was marketed in the USA in 1998 as part of a sports sponsorship campaign, selling only 200,000 cases. (Li, Shooshtari 2003)

Therefore, applying NLP principles would be a better approach in the branding process's building blocks to form a complete, multidimensional mental construct of the intended brand and its linguistic elements for a particular context.

Perceptual positions are described in NLP: The power of imagination.
See illustration below.
1st I see you.
2nd I see myself from your viewpoint, eyes.
3rd I see you and me.
4th I see you, me, and the 3rd position in combination from above.
Using this imaginative process, you can see different perspectives within a specific context to improve the communication process and delivery of a message or concept, i.e., does it fit?

Building a brand from its foundation using a priming approach or that of suggestion, we could apply the NLP perceptual positions approach to finding an appropriate fit and strategy to brand building (Ruch *et al.* 2016; Murphy[3]; Karam *et al.* 2017). This would entail thought processes at a multidimensional level to examine a product or brand effect on potential consumers. Let us consider a few points related to the senses, product placements, and product endorsements that may be below the threshold of awareness (Elgendi *et al.* 2018). To understand the idea priming or out-of-awareness methods of branding, we could consider the expression: *the hand is quicker than the eye*. In NLP, it is called the *sleight of hand*. It should be noted that the eye is, in fact, quicker than the hand, but the metaphor means to use a distraction technique or to do something not seen by the participant as to when playing cards. If the person playing the game is unaware of the methods being used or what the game is about, the methods employed are out of their awareness, thus under the threshold of their awareness or conscious perception. By knowing how to play the game, one will know the methods, actions, and cards to play.

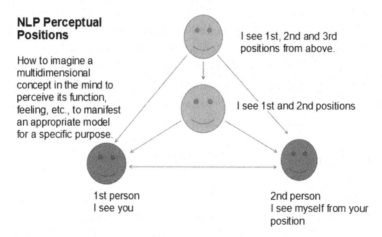

We could employ linguistic predicates in the communication or physical elements that may be under the threshold of awareness. Olfactory (smell) sensations like a subtle scent, kinesthetic (feel) vibratory

---

[3]Murphy, J. (2020). *The POWER of Your Subconscious Mind*, Vishakhapatnam: Andhra Research University.

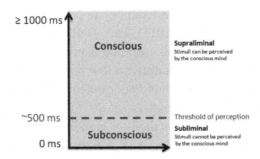

Figure 2. An illustration of supraliminal vs. subliminal priming. In subliminal priming, subjects are not aware of the stimuli as it occurs quickly (approximately less than 500 ms), yet it still influences them.

sensations, or even sounds since a vibration from a device can be felt, auditory (hear) cues such as low volume background music or visual (see) prompts such as product placements. These examples could be out of the consumers' awareness and still influence the purchase patterns of the buyer (Pollock 2016; Milliman 1986; Schouten *et al.* 2020; Knoll and Matthes 2016; Kramoliš and Kopečková 2013). Subliminal messaging is the priming of behavior outside of awareness when the receiving party has been exposed to stimuli below the threshold of perception, for example, in visual or auditory channels, where the stimuli may influence the decision-making process (Karam *et al.* 2017; Ruch *et al.* 2016). "This process occurs outside the realm of consciousness and is different from memory which relies on direct retrieval of information" (Elgendi *et al.* 2018, p. 1), as shown in Figure 2.

As we look further into word structure, we may begin to find greater possibilities in branding methods. Let us look more closely at some other commonly used words in the English language in business, such as *pharmacy's* etymology and phonology. By firstly looking at the pho-nological elements, one can notice p-*HARM*-acy. The word "harm" is generally considered a negative word and is slightly hidden in the spelling of *pharmacy* — which could be under the threshold of awareness or perception, i.e., the term visual priming (Elgendi *et al.* 2018). "P-*harm-acy*" also contradicts the general intention of what most would consider being a word for helping or improving one's health based on its etymology.[4]

> Pharmacy is derived from Greek *farmakeia*: use of drugs, medicines, potions, or spells; poisoning, witchcraft; from pharmakeus (fem. pharmakis): preparer of drugs, poisoner, sorcerer; from pharmakon: drug, poison, philter, charm, spell, enchantment; from pharmakós: (Greek: φαρμακός) in Ancient Greek religion was the ritualistic, sacrifice or exile of a human scapegoat or victim.[5]

The etymological definition does match the phonological element *harm*, regardless of the meaning that is generally accepted in modern times for *pharmacy*. We should consider that what we may accept as being one thing could be differently understood by researching more of the language used to define what something is as there are other parts of the meaning to perceive. By applying the methods and tools used in NLP, we will have more successful opportunities since we can analyze the elements and foundations of communication more precisely, and create others for branding purposes whether they are visible or not.

We have now introduced multiple NLP-based ideas and concepts that may be used to develop a brand via priming or out of awareness approaches within select contexts. The next section will cover some further elements to build a solid foundation for a brand.

This section suggests that there are deeper meanings to language based on codes. Communication may also be used in subtle ways to stimulate, and that words may not be transposable to different cultures.

---

[4]Online Etymology Dictionary. Pharmacy (n.). https://www.etymonline.com/word/pharmacy (accessed on July 17, 2020).
[5]Wikipedia. Pharmacos. https://en.wikipedia.org/wiki/Pharmakos) (accessed on July 18, 2020).

5. The Minute Language Structures That Govern an Idea and Meaning — A Word's Etymology

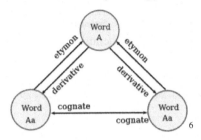

We know what words mean from their origin or *etymology:* "facts of the origin and development of a word",[7] as the image above shows. It would be advantageous to build a brand name from this approach since we could find all the possible meanings and associations in an attempt to determine whether the target consumer would be intrigued by it using the NLP methodology or even create one from scratch.

Let us use a common English word to find its true etymological meaning from its original Latin foundation. Take the word *government,* for instance. In Latin, "ment" means a general result of the action of thought, i.e., *mind.* "Govern" generally means *rule* or *control.* If a person supports *a government*, that person gives their consent to control by a third party's actions, or that is to say, they agree to *mind control*, based on that original meaning in Latin. Let us add the suffix *-al* to *government*:

mental (adj.)
early 15c., "in, of, or about the mind; characteristic of the intellect", from Late Latin *mentalis* "of the mind", from Latin *mens* (genitive *mentis*) "mind", from PIE root *men- (1) "to think".

In Middle English, also "of the soul, spiritual". From the 1520s as "done or performed in the mind". Meaning "crazy, deranged" is by 1927, probably from

[6]By Gufosowa — Own work. Etymology. Based on en:File: Etymological Relationships Tree.png, CC BY-SA 4.0. https://commons.wikimedia.org/w/index.php?curid=89059240 (accessed on November 8, 2020).
[7]Etymology Online Dictionary. Etymology (n.). https://www.etymonline.com/word/etymology (accessed on November 8, 2020).

combinations such as *mental patient* (1859); *mental hospital* (1891). *Mental health* is attested by 1803; *mental illness* by 1819; *mental retardation* by 1904.[8]

If -*al* is added to *ment* it becomes "*mental*", thus in Latin, it means or is related to a state of *mind*. If "*governmental organization*" were written as "*mind* or *mental retardation controlling body*" as but only one possibility, would the common person support it? What exactly *governs* a person in the world of business and society? The answer is the language and methods of communication used in marketing ideas.

Homophonic or the morphological (morphemes) structure of the English language also needs consideration in the brand-building process. The morpheme is the smallest meaningful linguistic unit of language, not divisible or analyzable into smaller forms (Zhang and Zhou 2013). Using the example of the word "compartmentalization" in the smallest language units is as follows: *Com-part-ment-al-iz-ation*. Each piece has a defined function and meaning that may be a mixture of many languages or even phonetic meanings.

In a paper regarding duel branding strategy for launching new products in China, Lam *et al.* (2013) use various examples of translating words from English to Chinese to have a suitable connection or cultural understanding of China's products, for example, Minute Maid branded goods. Lam *et al.* (2013) discuss how to translate and adapt *Minute Maid Orange Pulp* into the Chinese market. Another product is discussed related to snack foods with the possible name of *Potato "Zero" Chip (PZC)* or *"Zero" Potato Chip (ZPC)* where surveys were conducted to see how the names affected the participants (extracted from the table, p. 587); assuming zero means no quantity or number; naught.[9] What is worth discussing is the meaning of the words in the structures used in English. Thus, we could deduce that the structures mean a *potato with [no] chip* or *[no] potato chip*. Note the numerology of the letters used as well, PZC and ZPC are 9-26-3 and 26-9-3 positioning in the alphabet respectively, consisting of three words. We will cover more on "threes" later on in the chapter.

---

[8]Online Etymology Dictionary. Mental (adj.). https://www.etymonline.com/search?q=mental (accessed on July 17, 2020).

[9]Online Etymology Dictionary. Zero (n.). https://www.etymonline.com/word/zero (accessed on July 17, 2020).

Other intriguing points regarding the words used in branding, for example, Minute Maid: "minute" and "minute" are two different words in phonetic or homophonic meaning and the same in spelling, but the etymological meanings are many and generally are not related to the product in question. The former meaning "time" and the latter meaning "small". If we consider the other word "maid". *Made* is the past tense of the verb "make" and "maid" is a noun for a "servant". The combination of the two sets of words produces "Minute/Minute Maid/Made". The etymological meaning of 'maid' as defined:

maid (n.)

c. 1200 (late 12c. in place names and surnames), "an unmarried woman (usually young); the Virgin Mary;" shortening of maiden (n.). Like that word, used in Middle English of unmarried men as well as women (as in *maiden-man*, c. 1200, which was used of both sexes, reflecting also the generic use of *man*).

From c. 1300 as "a virgin", also as "maidservant, female attendant, lady in waiting". By c. 1500 this had yielded the humbler sense of "female servant or attendant charged with domestic duties". Often with a qualifying word (housemaid, chambermaid, etc.); *maid of all work* "female servant who performs general housework" is by 1790.[10]

We could say the brand means a *small female servant who performs general housework* as only one idea, but that may not function well in a brand. Thus, we could assume the structures' meaning could be more than four different concepts to the sets of words since the brain must deduce all possibilities, and none of them describe the actual product or connect to its contents.

A Tidbit of Wisdom

Earl Nightingale "Whatever we plant in our subconscious mind and nourish with repetition and emotion will one day become a reality". This suggests the programming of the person's mind and behavior by whatever form of communication.

---

[10]Online Etymology Dictionary. Maid (n.). https://www.etymonline.com/search?q=maid (accessed on July 17, 2020).

Based on the above definition, we could postulate the reason for *Minute Maid* vs. *Minute Made* as the former will intrigue the reader both unconsciously and consciously, spurring greater growth and development of the synapses in the neurological network.

Associating multiple ideas to the brand image, confusing or otherwise, while with surprise or a sense of confusion, but still legible to the senses, is what those word combinations suggest. The language used should also be culturally adaptable so that it would be acceptable, such as from the same family of language vs. a foreign one as the consumer may accept the suggestion. Considering the hierarchy of needs it is proposed that people are attracted to the mysterious, unknown, chaotic, unorganized, and unexplained (Maslow 1987). Once the foundation of words is precisely chosen, the structure or sentence then delivers the meaning, or the syntax, i.e., a linguistic program, to the receiver.[11]

We could conclude by saying that consumers would ultimately choose the brand image that sparks mystery, intrigue, excitement, and the possibility of the unknown, and may not describe or be associated with that good or service, which is planted deep in memory as long as it is culturally and linguistically suitable.

> This section covered the origin of words or etymology, how words have multiple meanings, the association of meanings to a word, and the synaptic network's spurring to a given idea for greater recall.

6. Numbers, Letters, Words, and a Mathematical Code of Geometry

When reading or listening to some unique sets of word groupings with multiple sensory perceptive meanings, the receiver may be taken to another state of mind or dimension by using metaphors, for example, which may be due to the numerologically significant numbers used and the multiple word meanings effects in select formation and structure, which could correlate to the Golden Ratio geometrical pattern (Lawrence 2001; Phillips 1992).

---

[11] Online Etymology Dictionary. Sentence (n.). https://www.etymonline.com/search?q=sentence (accessed on July 18, 2020).

This section touches on the premise that our reality is derived by a mathematical code that forms geometric shapes, frequencies, sounds *(language)*, and ultimately life as we know it. What if we could apply NLP methods to the mysterious code of numbers, sounds, and shapes to create a better brand? We argue that there are secrets in this reality, especially in the language itself; thus, the concept of numerology has a foundation in language structure. We will touch on a few points regarding numerology, while further research is needed to determine other relationships to the matters discussed in this section.

As we mentioned in the previous section, it was proposed that by using the examples of Minute/Minute Maid/Made (13-13) and "Zero" Potato Chip (PZC and ZPC are 16-26-3 and 26-16-3 in the alphabet, consisting of 3 words in each example), etc., the chosen words in these combinations have some mysterious form or feeling or a sense of confusion when reading them. When looking further at the words used in mass media, music, etc., we can begin to find commonalities and patterns of the employed words or that of numbers associated with them.

Using numerology as a starting point to find a foundation in using certain letters of the alphabet, Gillman explains:

> … For instance, the numbers 3, 6, and 9 have a special significance on this plane. The triangle has 3 sides, with angles equaling 180 degrees, divisible by 3, 6, and 9. The circle has 360 degrees, also divisible by 3, 6, and 9… Endless formulas, equations, and geometric images illustrate that these 3 numbers are paramount to the universe's grand design.[12]

If we look at some of the best-known symbols, logos, and designs used in marketing, we could begin to connect the idea of *circles* and *triangles*, both mathematically perfect. Nikola Tesla once said "If you only knew the magnificence of the 3, 6 and 9, then you would have the key to the universe".

---

[12]Gillman, J, H. Dream Time Code: The Alphabet Conspiracy. http://www.dreamtimecode.com/ (accessed on July 20, 2020).

We can also see the shapes used using these formulas and the language and frequencies in music. We should consider whether a word or the combination of words *restricts or expand*s the receiver's thinking process when seeing or listening to them. Gillman continues:

> The majority of films, television shows, products, magazines, stores, slogans, videogames, songs, and albums are titled to follow something called the "Rule of 3", defined as the great overuse of letters that contain a multiple of 3 according to their place in the alphabet. That means that most of the words you see every day in the mass media begin with C (letter 3), F (6), I (9), M (13), P (16), S (19), W (23), and Z (26). This, the "3" group, is also used with letters that act to support its power: A (1), B (2), J (10), K (11), and T (20), letters which contain 1 or 2. ... this "code" is an arcane subject worthy of unending study and contemplation. Every single media piece is meant to represent, in the letters and initials of its title, its themes. The "Rule of 3" is pervasive throughout the mass media because it also permeates through our physical plane of existence. The remaining letters are eschewed because they permeate through the higher, astral plane of existence, something which is rarely represented in the mainstream media.

The English philosopher and mathematician Newton (1642–1727) was the first to describe the mathematical synchronicity of color with music noting we will list key words, letters, and numbers tinted in grey for this publication (see Table 1). He was the one to discover the dispersion of white light into the prism of seven colors and assigned each of them to its corresponding musical tone (Lawrence 2001); note that the corresponding adding of colors to key words, letters, and numbers are in grey color tint to differentiate the respective entries in Tables 2 and 3.

A company could create a palindrome that uses all the letters within the tables shown. One such example is CITIC, which means China (3), International (9), Trust (2), Investment (9) and Corporation (3), summing up to 26.

> The palindrome is a type of wordplay involving the alphabet. A palindrome is a word, phrase or sentence that reads the same backward or forward — such as Madam, I'm Adam. Semordnilaps (the word palindromes in reverse) are words that spell other words when spelled backward (for

Table 1. Isaac Newton's mathematical synchronicity of color with music.

Red	Orange	Yellow	Green	Blue	Indigo	Violet
C	D	E	F	G	A	B
3	4	5	6	7	1	2

Source: Reader's Digest Great Encyclopedic Dictionary, p. 911, extracted from Lawrence 2001.

Table 2. Letters that act to support the group of three are known as "catalyst" groups. Random words were added for reference only and can be modified or changed to create new brand name combinations.

A	B	J	K	T
1	2	10	11	20
Alpha	Beta	Jackpot	King	Technology
Apple	Bureau	Jade	Kabob	Time
Amazing	Beautiful	Jazz	Kabuki	Tabernacle
Agency	Big	Just	Kabul	Trust
Am	Base	Jewel	Know	Trio

Table 3. Letters with the so-called group of three. Random words were added for reference only and can be modified or changed to create new brand name combinations.

C	F	I	M	P	S	W	Z
3	6	9	13	16	19	23	26
Corporation	Famous	Investment	Management	Principle	Show	Winner	Zeal
Creative	Freedom	International	Magical	Popular	Service	Wealth	Zany
Confident	Fabulous	Influential	Media	Professional	Superior	Wise	Zag
Caring	Free	Intrigue	Marvelous	Perfect	Sensational	Witty	zipper
China	Focus	Intelligence	Major	Proactive	Space	Whole	Zigzag
Central	Foreign	Investigation	Minute	Profit	Sensitive	White	Zealous

example, star/rats, drawer/reward). Palindrome Examples: pop, deed, kayak, civic, radar, level, deified, rotator, repaper, testset, racecar ...[13]

---

[13] Nordquist, R. Palindrome. https://www.thoughtco.com/what-is-a-palindrome-1691560 (accessed on January 11, 2020).

We can expand on this with NLP predicates that are sensory-based to create a brand image. The words are randomly listed in their key numerological position in the alphabet with color added for Newton's mathematical synchronicity with music based on the previous tables. NLP suggests that each person has their preference of language patterns based on visual, auditory, kinesthetic, olfactory, gustatory channels to understand and communicate with. The choice of words used may attract or deter the consumer based on the sensory representation used, that is to say, is the message sent in *rapport* with the receiver? (see Table 4).

For example, if a Chinese SME is producing food products, then *TMT* (To My Taste) could be a brand (or a slogan) that appeals to smell and taste-related sensory channels. Another example could be *It Clicks* (means to immediately like someone or something); *CCA* (Crystal Clear Acoustics); or *SAB* (Sparkling Acoustic Balance) for an instrument manufacturer since it is an auditory channel and may have a kinesthetic sensation to it as well. Another method would be to find keywords with multiple etymological phonological meanings and create a table to select, merge or create new words that may suit the target market for the brand creation. We could add various words to those select letter groups to create new words, names, mottoes or slogans based on a variety of characteristics that may fit the prescribed conditions described in the paper.

Noting the number "3" or the *rule of three* as key, there is great evidence that threes may have some form of special significance in the world since it is seen or used in various ways using acronyms and initialisms such as the top three companies in each sector or with the following brands or organizational names: MandM (26), CIA (13), FBI (17), BoA (3), BoC (5), BYD (31), etc., and in all walks of life, in plants and shapes in nature. Gillman continues:

> ... the preposition "of" is used to assert that one entity is related to and part of another. In all other cases, the initials of words are what matters. However, as used by The Code, "of" does not signify O (15), but instead implies a correlative relationship between the initials on its two sides. ... Every initial is either a "3" letter, those containing a multiple of 3 according to their place in the alphabet, or is part of the "catalyst" group, those containing 1 or 2. The word "of" solidifies a connection between the initials which it intersects.

Table 4. NLP-based predicate table with selected color and numerology significant numbers.

	Visual Predicates		Auditory Predicates		Kinesthetic Predicates		Olfactory and Gustatory Predicates
1	Appear	1	Acoustic	2	Balanced	2	Bitter
2	Blurred	2	Blast	3	Cold	6	Fragrant
2	Brilliant	3	Calls	6	Feel	19	Seasoning
3,3	Crystal clear	3	Chanting	6	Firmly	19	Stinking
3	Clarify	7	Harmony	7	Grasp	19	Sweet
3	Color	7	Hear	7	Gripping	19	Smell
3	Colorful	9,3	It clicks		Heartbreaking	20	Tasteful
6	Focus		Listening		Heartwarming	20,13,20	To my taste
6	Foreseen		Loud (and clear)		Heated (heated debate)		
9	Illustrate	13	Melody		Hold		
9	Insight		Outspoken		Light-footed		
16	Perspective		Questions	13	Moving		
	Review		Roar	19	Slipped		
19	See	19	Say	19	Slowly…		
19	Sharp	19	Screaming	19	Solid		
19	Shiny	19	Shout	19	Support		
19	Sparkling	19	Sound Acoustic	20	Tangibly		
	Uncover	20	Talking	20	Transform		
	View	20	Tuning/tuning in	23	Warm		
	Vision		Voice	23	Wet		

Throughout history, inventors such as Galileo Galilei, Nikola Tesla, and Leonardo DaVinci have all refereed to maths, language, shapes, and symbols in their works:

Philosophy [nature] is written in that great book which ever is before our eyes — I mean the universe — but we cannot understand it if we do not first learn the language and grasp the symbols in which it is written. The book is written in mathematical language, and the symbols are triangles, circles and other geometrical figures, without whose help it is impossible to comprehend a single word of it; without which one wanders in vain through a dark labyrinth.[14]

The general premise suggested is that math or numbers, which can be associated with language and music, can and does create a sense of illusion within the mind depending on how select words and structure are produced in a given context as suggested here:

Sacred geometry is another term for the Algorithm, Matrix, Illusion, or Simulation that unites and creates all realities. Sacred geometry involves sacred universal patterns used in everything in our reality, most often seen in sacred architecture and sacred art. The basic belief is that geometry and mathematical ratios, harmonics, and proportion are also found in music, light, cosmology. This value system is seen as widespread even in prehistory, a cultural universal of the human condition.[15]

The Golden Ratio or *phi* may balance all proportions in art or drawing and design as a final point of this section. Language and the images used in advertising and branding are crucial to a successful business, and thus the firm building a brand image should factor in such geometric shapes and ideas when building the brand:

The Golden ratio was used to achieve balance and beauty in many Renaissance paintings and sculptures. Da Vinci himself used the Golden ratio to define all of the proportions in his Last Supper, including the table's dimensions and the proportions of the walls and backgrounds. The Golden ratio also appears in da Vinci's Vitruvian Man and the Mona Lisa.[16]

The next section will show how some of the previous language and structure topics are used in stories, marketing, and business in general and

---

[14]Goodreads. Galileo Galilei. Retrieved July 20, 2020. https://www.goodreads.com/quotes/28019-philosophy-nature-is-written-in-that-great-book-which-ever.

[15]Crystal Links. Sacred Geometry. Retrieved July 20, 2020. https://www.crystalinks.com/sg.html.

[16]Bugged Space. Nikola Tesla 3 6 9 Theory and Why he called it Key To Universe. Posted, September 29, 2019. https://www.buggedspace.com/tesla-3-6-9-theory-and-why-he-called-it-key-to-universe/.

their ability to attract, involve, hook, and lead the receiver by using various NLP techniques.

We covered some general aspects of numerology, maths, geometry, colors, and concepts such as The Golden Rule, which may affect the human mind by creating a matrix of some form using various combinations of words and structures, affecting the human thinking process.

---

7. The Structure of Imaginary Intent — Mind Digests the Message to Seek a Conclusion

As we look into the concept of programming or that of linguistics, we can see that the power of language in communication is greater than many may *realize* (is a visual predicate and its phonetic breakdown is real-ize or real eyes). This section will show how association, anchoring, suggestion, and figurative language structures in branding can be used to create an intriguing connection to a good or service.

Years ago, I and some colleagues superimposed new concepts to commonly known words to form company names and trademarks in our business activities. For example, "etc.", which is pronounced "et cetera" in Latin and means "and the others". The meaning we associated to *etc.* was *education, translation, consulting*, and adding *network*, we got "etc network" as the company name. We decided to use "etc" (which can be pronounced e-t-c) since it is used daily in written and spoken communication. Thus, we associated *etc.* with the company name to achieve greater brand awareness. We created the slogan "The little big network" to suggest extensive resources using the [oxymoron] *little big* as it was a small operation with 8 full-time staff and over 80 freelancers. Noting that *little* was a smaller font size while *big* was a larger one to impress the larger idea than what we appeared to be.

In the before-mentioned trademark infringement case, the name we chose was *"Andale!"*, pronounced "An-da-lé", which in the Mexican language means "hurry up" or "let's go", for the energy drink brand and company name. In English, someone would say "An-dale". The brand name suggests the concept of movement or energy "speed", which would make logical sense for that business model. The concept was designed and marketed towards the Latino American segment using various associated characteristics such as graphics, flavors, and sports (soccer). You may gain more attention by associating the brand with known expressions and associations to a specific target demographic since many people are familiar with those particular words or structures, even when using non-English terms in an English-speaking market. We used the metaphor *"Join in the Revolution, Andale!"* as the slogan. Noting that most native English speakers know basic Mexican words from TV and school and thus it is an acceptable foreign language to use in the US market.

Our branding campaign associated "Andale!" to mean energy drink. There are various methods and techniques available to associate something new to an existing concept while even using a foreign language in a domestic market as long as it is comprehensible or could be associated to the local language and culture as we have shown. *Rapido!* (ra-pi-do), which means quickly in Mexican, was also used for an energy shot in the family of drinks created by the Andale! company. Thus, *Andale! Rapido!* (let's go — quickly) was the shot's brand name.

Figurative language may be used to compare two unlike ideas to increase understanding of one, which corroborates the Helegian Dialectic[17] model; to show a deeper emotion or connection to something or someone; assist in visualization and to elicit emotion, which all should stimulate the neuro-synaptic networks for improved long-term memory. Figurative language consists of simile, metaphor, personification, onomatopoeia, oxymoron, hyperbole, litotes, idiom, alliteration, and allusion.

There are many examples of figurative language mentioned that could be applied to building a brand image. This short story is to illustrate some NLP structures that could be applied in select branding processes such as how your business was started (emphasis added):

> … *one time* I was strolling through central park on my way home … when all of a sudden a *little big*, beautiful woman who looked *as strong as an ox*

---

[17] Stanford Encyclopedia of Philosophy, Hegel's Dialectics. Retrieved November 2, 2020. First published Fri Jun 3, 2016; substantive revision Fri Oct 2, 20 https://plato.stanford.edu/entries/hegel-dialectics/.

silently approached me ... *can you imagine that now*? I was so *frightened and excited* at the same time, *you know*, and she asked me a question and I responded ... *And then we went home* ...

We could assume there are various associations that most people would have experienced and placed in long-term memory during their life in this story (strolling, park, surprise, frightened, excited, home, etc.). There are also references to how fairy-tales are told as well (one time = once upon a time/and then we went home = we lived happily ever after) that would connect or place the listener/reader in the form of an emotionally memorable state of mind established neuro-synaptic networks as most kids are told the same lines repeatably in childhood. Using an oxymoron, a metaphor, a hyperbole, a simile, etc., can enhance the association and intrigue for the target audience of a brand to engage neuro-synaptic networks and emotional responses.

We could use a structure such as: "And then we went home..." which could mean together or separate, but it lacks that definitive information to answer the question. We could assume the reader would think they went home together, but the point is that vagueness creates *interest or intrigue or that of fantasy* in the receiver's mind since there is no clear mention of who went where with whom. This method could be used in a company storyline to create intrigue for the consumer.

Using a suggestion structure *can you imagine that now* in branding communication, the receiver will have a profound involvement within the context described. Another expression that attracts the listener or reader is *you know*, which generally is a question needing a response; and using double suggestions in one message (frightened and excited simultaneously), which cause a sense of confusion. Let us take a look at the structure of this NLP suggestion:

Can (helping verb; meaning able); You (pronoun); Imagine (a verb; to see, visualize).

A simple sentence is:
    Can you imagine? (which is rather a command to think.)
We are now adding an idea or suggestion such as an elephant and pink in color.

> *Can you imagine a pink elephant?*

Furthermore, a verb is added for action — dancing.

> *Can you imagine a pink elephant dancing?*

Next, the inducer of time, such as *now*, would start the program.

> *Can you imagine a pink elephant dancing now?*

We can suggest and anchor meaning to a brand in the following manner. Let us first understand what anchoring is in NLP, which means associating one idea to another via a sensory channel such as sound, sight, etc., and as Pavlov's experiments had shown with a bell to link feeding time or food. The anchoring/suggestion formula is as follows:

(the method used to convey brand image) plus ("can you imagine") plus (sensory anchor: see, feel, hear, smell, taste) = association of brand image to (a) sensory channel(s) at the climax of imaginary experience of the message being delivered to the recipient. The anchor's introduction is crucial so that it is not too late or early to achieve the greatest synaptic stimulation and growth in the receiver's mind to the anchor since they are emotionally connecting the message to their personal experiences. Moreover, each time they experience that anchor, their memory should engage the brand.

When using the suggestion, *can you imagine* a [program] is planted in the receiver's mind so that they attempt to perceive the suggestion, which is called a *command inducer, i.e., a program starter in NLP terms.* That inducer forces the receiver to create a motion picture (cartoon) in their mind of the object (an elephant). By adding *now* at the end of the sentence, one is forced to think immediately as the program's time is stated and thus the program starts.

Another consideration is how negation, repetition, and certain word/letter combinations can change the meaning of word structures when used in a certain way in the following example of *"Don't, stop"*. By repeating this structure multiple times in a row, the meaning changes to "continue". While another example is the noun "space"; by adding the letter "x" to it, we get *spacex*. If "spacex" is repeated many times, it changes to "*spacesex*", which could also be the (visual or phonetic) connotation of "spasex", not to mention the rocket connection. The pronunciation of words and structure can affect the receiver in various ways, and thus the message that is to be remembered or used could be highlighted or even hidden when branding and advertising.

The final section will conclude this chapter and provide some possible suggestions as to how Chinese SMEs may approach building their international operations or product lines using some of the ideas introduced in NLP.

What can be learned from this section is that there are multiple methods to learn something, how stories are compelling with hidden meanings, and various structures and methods of programming to the unsuspected receiver.

---

8. Concluding Remarks

We endeavor to build a brand based on the neurological branding maxim that will spur the synaptic network to engage, use and expand continuously in the consumers' minds. We covered various marketing theories and practices, their approach and use, many practical examples of language, its etymology, numerology, how memory is formed, transpositioned, how the consumer may perceive words, and a host of other concepts that could be used to assist in the establishment of a footing in new or existing markets. The challenges that Chinese-based SMEs face in the international marketplace and the pressures of the market forces that prevail in cross-border business pose many obstacles for various reasons. Thus, having a solid foundation of linguistics' neurology may play a crucial role in establishing a successful brand.

Markets are dynamic systems governed and regulated by language, law, culture, tradition, rumor, agendas, consumption, and the concept of money and profitability or even greed. How to manage the many challenges and other factors that will inhibit the business plan and brand image creation and management? By using the scientific approach to the marketing of goods and services based on the neurological branding maxim of NLP and applying some of the options we covered in this chapter, Chinese SMEs can create a unique brand image that will be profitable and enduring if it can adapt to the local, cultural, and linguistic challenges being faced in that particular context. Noting the key factor is mastering the acquisition of the local communication styles and cultural characteristics of that target market while also knowing the procedures and steps to establish and manage the brand image holistically. In other words, a company needs to create a meta-model representation of the brand image that appeals to the target consumer in a metaphorically and emotionally created message that will attract or inspire them and connect to their inner world, which will spur them to purchase or consume the good or service.

As a final note, the brand is the key to doing business anywhere. Invest in neuro-linguistics elements and know that the market has many invisible hands that may hit the brand any time and in any place. Nevertheless, by adopting a flexible approach and becoming aware of the obstacles that such hidden challenges become expected, and aware the established competitive players influence the market far more than is told, the chances of success will be greater than taking the naive approach. Become distinctive and highly specialized like a *chameleon* to adapt to any market and deliver a *sensory brand image* identity to attract the consumer, linking that good or service to live happily ever after ...

Acknowledgment

Special thanks to my wife Angela for her patience and for critically commenting on my grammar, Chris Eckhardt for his contributions and perspectives on the approach of this chapter, and thousands that I have worked with and met across the world for giving me insight.

References

Bandler, R. and Grinder, J. (1975). *The Structure of Magic*, Palo Alto: Science and Behavior Books.

Basciano, B. (2016). *A Linguistic Overview of Brand Naming in the Chinese-Speaking World. (Università Ca' Foscari Venezia, Italia.)*, Vol. 52. Annali di Ca' Foscari. Serie orientale. pp. 243–296.

Bass, F. M. and Talarzyk, W. W. (1972). An attitude model for the study of brand preference, *Journal of Marketing Research*, 9(1), 93–96.

Blythe, J. (2000). *Marketing Communications*. Harlow: Pearson Education Ltd.

Brown, N. and Turnbull, J. (2000). Neuro-linguistic programming (NLP) and its relevance to effective communication. *ACCA Students Newsletter*, September, 4–9.

Brown, S. P. and Stayman, D. M. (1992). Antecedents and consequences of attitude toward the ad: A meta-analysis, *Journal of Consumer Research*, 19(June), 34–51.

Chiang, S.-Y. (2009). Interformative meaning of signs: Brand naming and globalization in China, *Social Semiotics*, 19(3), 329–344.

Coffey, G. and Phillips, B. (2010). *7 Seconds to Success*, Minneapolis: Mill City Press, Inc.

Cui, Y. (2019). The presentation of brand personality in English-Chinese brand name translation, *International Journal of Market Research*, 61(1), 33–49.

Elgendi, M., Kumar, P., Barbic, S., Howard, N., Abbott, D., and Cichocki, A. (2018). Subliminal priming — State of the art and future perspectives, *Journal of Behavioral Sciences MDPI*, 8, 54.

Engel, J. F., Warsaw, M. R., and Kinnear, T. C. (1994). *Promotional Strategy*, Chicago, IL: Irwin.

Gontijo, P. and Zhang, S. (2007). The mental representation of brand names: Are brand names a class by themselves? In *Psycholinguistic Phenomena in Marketing Communications*, ed. T. Lowery, pp. 23–37. Mahwah, NJ: Lawrence Erlbaum.

Gordon, W. (2002). Brands on the Brain: New Scientific Discoveries to Support New Brand Thinking. In *Brand New Brand Thinking*, eds. M. Baskin and M. Earls. pp. 103–121. London: Kogan Page.

Hovland, C. I., Janis, I. L., and Kelly, H. H. (1953). *Communication and Persuasion*, New Haven (CT): Yale University Press.

Karam, R., Haidar, M., Abbas Khawaja, A., and Laziki, G. (2017). Effectiveness of subliminal messages and their influence on people's choices, *European Scientific Journal*, 13(17), p. 262.

Keller, K. L. and Lehmann, D. R. (2006). Brands and branding: Research findings and future priorities, *Marketing Science*, 25(6), 740–759.

Knoll, J. and Matthes, J. (2016). The effectiveness of celebrity endorsements: A meta-analysis, *Department of Communication*, 45, 55–75.

Kotler, P. (2001). *A Framework for Marketing Management*, Upper Saddle River: Prentice-Hall.

Kotler, P. and Keller, K. L. (2012). *Marketing Management*, 14th ed., New Jersey: Pearson Prentice Hall.

Kramoliš, J. and Kopečková, M. (2013). Product placement: A smart marketing tool shifting a company to the next competitive level, *Journal of Competitiveness*, 5(4), 98–114.

Lam, P. Y., Chan, A., Gopaoco, H., Oh, K., and So, T. H. (2013). *Dual Branding Strategy for a Successful New Product Launch in China*, Indiana: Kelley School of Business, Indiana University, Elsevier Inc.

Lavidge, R. J. and Steiner, G. A. (1961). A model for predictive measurements of advertising effectiveness, *Journal of Marketing Research*, 25(October), 59–62.

Lawrence, S. B. and Msc. D. (2001). *The Secret Science of Numerology: The Hidden Meaning of Numbers and Letters*. Wayne: The Career Press, Inc.

Li, F. and Shooshtari, N. H. (2003). Multinational Business Review, ISSN 1525-383X.

Li, Y. and Zhao, M. (2018). Must the underdog win? The moderation effect of product type in the underdog effect of brand stories, *Asian Journal of Social Psychology*, 21, 237–245.

MacKenzie, S. B., Lutz, R. J., and Belch, G. E. (1986). The role of attitude toward the ad as a mediator of advertising effectiveness: A test of competing explanations, 23, 130–143.

McGuire, W. J. An Information Processing Model of Advertising Effectiveness. In *Behavioral and Management Science in Marketing*, eds. Davis, H. L., Silk, A. J., pp. 156–180, New York: Ronald Press.

Miller, D. W., Hadjimarcou, J., and Miciak, A. (2000). A scale for measuring advertisement-evoked mental imagery, *Journal of Marketing Communications*, 6, 1–20.

Milliman, R. (1986). The influence of background music on the behavior of restaurant patrons, *Journal of Consumer Research*, 13(2), 286–289.

Mitchell, A. and Olson, J. (1981). Are product attribute beliefs the only mediator of advertising effects on brand attitudes? *Journal of Marketing Research*, 18, 318–332.

Nutley-Smith, K. (1997). *The Hypnotic Manager*, London: Rushmere Wynne Limited.

O'Connor, J. and Seymour, J. (1994). *Training with NLP*, London: Thorsons.

Phillips, D. A. (1992). *The Complete Book of Numerology*, Hay House, Inc.

Pollock, C. (2016). The canary in the coal mine, *Journal of Avian Medicine and Surgery*, 30(4), 386–391.

Ramón, D., Cortésl, E., and Garcíal, L. (2016). Chinese multinationals in Spain: Determinants of establishment mode choice. *University of Alicante (Spain)*. N° de clasificación.

Ruch, S., Zust, M., and Henke, K. (2016). Subliminal messages exert long-term effects on decision-making, *Neuroscience of Consciousness*, 2016(1), 1–9.

Sawyer, A. G. (1981). Repetition, cognitive responses, and persuasion. In *Cognitive Responses in Persuasion*, eds. R. E. Petty, T. M. Ostrom, and T. C. Brock, pp. 237–262, Hillsdale (NJ): Erlbaum.

Schmitt, B. H. (1994). Corporate and brand identities in the Asia-Pacific region: Theoretical and applied perspectives. In *AP — Asia Pacific Advances in Consumer Research*, eds. Cote, J. A. and Leong, S. M., Vol. 1, pp. 1–3. Provo, UT: Association for Consumer Research.

Schouten, A. P., Janssen L., and Verspaget, M. (2020). Celebrity vs. influencer endorsements in advertising: The role of identification, credibility, and product-endorser fit, *International Journal of Advertising*, 39(2), 258–281.

Sheena, N. (2012). Do brand personalities make a difference to consumers? *Procedia: Social and Behavioral Sciences*, 37, 31–37.

Sheth, J. N. and Rajendra, S. S. (2002). *The Rule of Three: Surviving and Thriving in Competitive Markets*, New York: NY, Free Press.

Skinner, H. and Stephens, P. (2003). Speaking the same language: The relevance of neuro-linguistic programming to effective marketing communications, *The Journal of Marketing Communications*, 9, 177–192.

Su, F., Khan, Z., Lew, Y. K., Park, B. I., and Choksy, U. S. (2020). Internationalization of Chinese SMEs: The role of networks and global value chains, *Business Research Quarterly*, 23(2), 141–158.

Tian, K. and Dong, L. (2011). *Consumer-Citizens of China: The Role of Foreign Brands in the Imagined Future of China*, London: Routledge.

Trusov, M., Bucklin, R. E., and Pauwels, K. (2009). Effects of word-of-mouth versus traditional marketing: Findings from an internet social networking site, *Journal of Marketing*, 73(5), 90–102.

Walvis, T. H. (2008). Three laws of branding: Neuroscientific foundations of effective brand building, *Brand Management*, 16(3), 176–194.

Wilson, W. R. (1979). Feeling more than we can know: Exposure effects without learning, *Journal of Personality and Social Psychology*, 37(June), 811–821.

Yoo, B. and Donthu, N. (2001). Developing and validating a multidimensional consumer-based brand equity scale, *Journal of Business Research*, 52(1), 1–14.

Zajonc, R. B. (1980). Feeling and thinking: Preferences need no inferences, *American Psychologist*, 35, 151–175.

Zhang, Y. and Zhou, X. (2013). *An Introduction to Modern English Lexicology*, Beijing: Normal University Press.

Index

Printed in the United States
by Baker & Taylor Publisher Services